D1175098

Books by Dr. Ernest A. Fitzgerald

HOW TO BE A SUCCESSFUL FAILURE

THERE'S NO OTHER WAY

THE STRUCTURES OF INNER PEACE

YOU CAN BELIEVE

LIVING UNDER PRESSURE

*How to Be a
Successful Failure*

Dr. Ernest A. Fitzgerald

How to Be a
Successful Failure

New York 1978 ATHENEUM/SMI

Library of Congress Cataloging in Publication Data
Fitzgerald, Ernest A
    How to be a successful failure.

    "An Atheneum/SMI book."
    1. Failure (Psychology) I. Title.
BF575.F14F57   158'.1   77-13463
ISBN 0-689-10842-7

Published simultaneously in Canada by McClelland and
Stewart, Ltd.
Manufactured by American Book-Stratford Press, Inc.
Saddle Brook, New Jersey
Designed by Kathleen Carey
First Edition

To Aunt Fronie

A WINNER IN EVERYTHING THAT COUNTED

With Appreciation

To my wife, Frances, who spends a lot of lonely evenings while her husband struggles with paper and pen. She reads what is written, and her suggestions are always helpful.

To my secretary, Mrs. David Lewis, whose vast knowledge of techniques and grammatical construction makes all my writing a pleasure.

To Mrs. Walter E. Johnson, Jr., who edits every page with wisdom and skill.

To the staff and 3,600 members of Centenary United Methodist Church in Winston-Salem, North Carolina, who constantly strive to help their minister be a winner even when he loses.

To Fisher-Harrison Corporation, publishers of PACE,

With Appreciation

the inflight magazine of Piedmont Airlines, for per-
mission to reprint much of the material in Chapter 1,
and which allows me to be a regular contributor to
its publication.

To many unnamed and sometimes unknown people
who have shared with me some of the ideas in this
little book. For me, each one of them is a champion.

Ernest A. Fitzgerald
Winston-Salem, N.C.

Foreword

SOMEONE has said that the most encouraging news to be found in any newspaper is on the sports page. Here you find stories of the winners and the records of those who have excelled where the competition is keen and the games are played by champions. For the most part, that is true. But it is no less true that the sports page has its sad stories, too. For every winner there is a loser, and everyone who makes it to the top leaves someone at the bottom.

Books are alive with the glamorous records of the stars, but little is written about the man or woman who walks the low road. A leading educator recently said, "Everyone wants to write a book on how to succeed. No one seems to be saying anything about how to handle failure. Yet most of us will lose more often than we will win."

That observation was not totally accurate. It is true, however, that Americans are heavily oriented toward success. The businessman pushes for the top; the student is pressured to rank first in his class; and the housewife feels compelled to travel in the best social circles. We are all "under the gun" to succeed. The trouble is, a lot of us don't! How do we handle it when we are not No. 1?

This book is dedicated to the losers—to those who don't make it to stardom. Its purpose is to look at some of the strategic events in every person's life, and to remind us that we can win, even when we lose.

Wander through its pages. Perhaps, somewhere, you'll find your name.

Contents

xi

How to Be a
Successful Failure

How to Be a
Successful Failure

A FEW years ago one of the national television networks carried the opening ceremonies at the restored Ford Theater in Washington, D.C. Just over a hundred years ago, this theater was the scene of one of the most far-reaching events in American history. On the evening of April 14, 1865, just five days after Lee's surrender at Appomattox, Abraham Lincoln was shot by a deranged actor named John Wilkes Booth. A century later on the opening night in the restored theater, the box in which Lincoln and his party had been seated was empty. This was fitting symbolism of the irreplaceable position Lincoln holds in American history.

As the television cameras roamed across those vacant seats, one could not help but remember that they appeared as silent witnesses to the unfinished dreams, the incompleted plans, and the unrealized hopes of the Great Emancipator. Lincoln felt his work hardly done, even though the war was over. In this regard Lincoln is a kindred spirit to most of us. Who ever has time to get everything done or to finish the proposed plans of life? The world is full of people who, for one reason or another, miss the goals they intended to reach.

Perhaps for this very reason, book publishers in recent years have been selling books on success. The currents of American thinking have been saturated with an endless parade of do-it-yourself plans for making it to the top. The theme is that success is guaranteed if one will only follow the simple instructions of hard work, of proper thinking, and of learning how to manipulate people and circumstances.

But for so many people these formulas have not worked. For most, the romanticism of the famed American success story always seems to happen to someone else. The brutal truth is that most of us know more about failure than we know about success. We feel we are losers in the battles we try to fight.

I'm a minister, and a lot of my time is spent behind the counselor's desk. There, I keep meeting people who have missed their mark. Sometimes they deserve to fail, because they haven't really tried or have ignored the discipline necessary to reach their goals; it requires no expert analysis to understand their problem. But there is another kind of failure not so easily understood. There are people who have done their best and *still* missed the target. The question they ask is always the same: "Why?"

What kind of answer is there for these people? Life is a complicated business—to suggest otherwise would be dishonest. Yet some things about failure are so obvious they are often overlooked. Consider three ideas.

First, failure is always relative to perspective. There is an old Norwegian tale about a fisherman who, with his two sons, went out on a daily fishing run. The catch was good; but by midafternoon a sudden storm blotted out the shoreline, leaving the men groping for the direction of home. Meanwhile, a fire broke out in the kitchen of their rustic cottage. Before it could be extinguished, the fire had destroyed the family's earthly possessions. Finally, the father and sons were able to row their boat ashore. The man's wife was waiting to tell him the tragic news of the fire. "Karl, fire has destroyed everything," she said tearfully. "We have nothing left." But Karl was unmoved by the news. "Didn't you hear me, Karl?" she asked. "The house is gone!" "Yes, I hear you," replied Karl. "But a few hours ago we were lost at sea. For hours I thought we would perish. Then something happened: I saw a dim yellow glow in the distance. It grew larger and larger. We turned our boat toward the light. The blaze that destroyed our home was the light that saved our lives."

Little commentary is needed on the lesson of that story. Failure often becomes success when seen from a different point of view.

History is full of this kind of thing. Columbus, looking for a new route to India, failed in his intended mission but unintentionally discovered a new world. In 1872 a severe hot spell in California shriveled a farmer's entire grape crop. He sent his dried-up grapes to a grocer who advertised them as "Peruvian Delicacies." They sold at a good price, and we've been eating raisins ever since. Failure is largely determined by your point of view. It is almost impossible to think of anything, no matter how bad, that doesn't have some good in it—if you look for it.

Second, failure is relative to our use of it. No one

can evaluate the place of any eventuality in life. Whether it is good or bad depends on how a circumstance is used. In John Wooden's autobiography, *They Call Me Coach*, there are a couple of particularly meaningful lines: "Things turn out best for those who make the best of the way things turn out." About a hundred years ago in Tuscumbia, Alabama, a nineteen-month-old child was deprived of sight and hearing. The child soon became mute. Yet, twenty-four years later, this child graduated *cum laude* from Radcliffe College. Since then, Helen Keller's closed eyes have opened the eyes of millions. There are times when the blind *can* lead the blind. Helen Keller did so. Beethoven's deaf ears have helped multitudes to hear immortal music. Catherine Marshall's broken heart made Peter Marshall immortal. Nothing is good or bad within itself. Value has some relationship to use. The worst can be made to serve the best purposes—if we know how to utilize it.

Third, failure is relative to time. Did you ever consider the fact that no one really knows when he has had a "good" day? Wallace Hamilton tells an old story about a Chinese landowner who had a large estate. One day some wild horses wandered on to his property. The horses were worth a fortune. The neighbors gathered to congratulate him on his good luck. The man stoically remarked,

"How do you know I am lucky?" Later the man's son was trying to break one of the horses. The boy was thrown, and his leg was broken. The neighbors tried to console the father on his misfortune. He asked again, "How do you know I have been unfortunate?" A while later the king declared war, and the landowner's son was exempted from military duty because of his broken leg. The neighbors came in to say how fortunate the man was. He asked the same question: "How do you know I am fortunate?"

How do we really know when we have had a good day? All of us have looked back on some happy experiences that seemed good at the time. But sometimes those experiences have later turned out to be not quite so happy. We have had some bad days, but far down the road we have been compelled to say, "It seemed terrible at the time, but as I look back, it was the best thing that ever happened to me." Time turns a lot of failures into successes. The fact is, you never really know when you have failed. Those empty chairs in that Washington theater have new meaning now. Time has fixed that life which ended so tragically into an immortal place in history. The loser has become the winner.

We need some new standards by which we may measure success. Genuine success does not always mean climbing to the top of the heap. I know a lot of people who have "arrived," and they are not very happy. Success is taking what life hands you and managing it so that, win, lose, or draw, you may look back and not be ashamed. That's what the rest of this book is about.

Handling Decisions

A PROFESSOR in a leading southern university spoke recently to a symposium studying the need for revision in the curriculum of schools and colleges. He suggested that, in days when the complexity of life leads to bewildering confusion among even the wisest minds, there is a need for intensive study in the process of decision making. The professor labeled the new course "Guessology" and felt that it should be offered independently of other academic disciplines. The subject matter of such a course would deal with making decisions when the choices must be determined by guess or calculated risks.

This proposal, apparently made in jest, may have considerable merit. Many of us are interested in relevant education, and the business of making up our minds in our kind of world is a real and practical problem.

Any counselor working directly with people continually meets folk who have difficulties making decisions. Life has a way of thrusting us into situations where decisions have to be made even though the issues are not clear. Young people in particular are squarely up against that predicament these days. At a recent science seminar, a research specialist declared that more than half of the vocational options for the future have not yet been identified. What he was saying is that many of the jobs that will be available in the next decade do not now exist. A young person thus finds himself in the untenable position of preparing himself for a world that has not yet come into being.

The youth of today, however, are not alone in their confrontation with uncertainty. Business people are compelled to chart the course of their businesses in the troubled waters of economic instability. Even parents feel inadequate to make wise decisions in a world so radically different from their own that the old guidelines seem obsolete. Every day in my work I talk with people who are struggling with one of two very real-life situations. Some have had to make a decision. Subsequent events have made it clear that they guessed wrong, and that the miscalculation has had far-reaching impact on their life. There are others who face the necessity of decision and are uncertain about their ability to make an intelligent choice. It's a tough place to live—that no man's land clouded either by a bad decision or by a choice you don't know how to make. The college professor was on target when he said that the problem of life in these turbulent years is how to make a choice and be sure the choice is right. Suppose you had to teach that course. What principles would you consider as important?

You would have to begin with the premise that to live is to decide. The decision-making process is an inherent part of the human situation.

Far back in the philosophical and theological reflection of man, there is an old notion called "predestination." In substance, the idea is that the course of life is predetermined either by the creative process or by some supernatural power over which man exercises little or no control. You often hear people saying, "It was meant to happen this way," or "Fate decided it for me," or even, "You won't die until your number is up." To some degree such attitudes about life are valid because it is true that we do not exercise complete control over what happens to us. But even the most ardent believer in a "fixed future" sometimes doesn't seem fully convinced that this is the way it has to be. There is an old story about a trapeze artist who was asked by his publicity agent to roll a wheelbarrow across a cable stretched over Niagara Falls. The high-wire artist hesitated, saying that it could be dangerous. But the agent insisted. "Don't worry about it. You won't die until your time comes." "Guess you are right," said the trapeze expert. "Tell you what: I'll roll the wheelbarrow if you will ride in it." The stunt never came off, and the reason is obvious: Most people are not willing to leave everything to fate when their lives are at stake. Deep down inside, we suspect that we *do* have a hand in what happens to us.

Did you ever wonder why we feel this way? An English theologian once suggested that when the Creator allots man his native equipment, this very equipment suggests something of what is expected of him. The fact that we have eyes implies that we are expected to see. Our ears suggest that we are to hear. That we have minds capable of discerning options suggests that we are intended to think and to choose. This argument is not without point. To be a person is to be a decision maker.

Of course, in many ways it would be a relief to evade the responsibilities of choice—especially when the problems are complicated. We don't mind handling the little things, but nothing exhausts our energies as does the laborious task of making a decision when the stakes are high. Our blood pressure goes up; our digestive system gets upset; and our nights are less than restful. It's a hard matter to make decisions when the columns don't add up and the options are unclear. But no one ever successfully evades the responsibility. To live means to make up your mind. It's a basic principle of human existence: We *are* decision makers.

But now let's move another step in our course on Guessology. Decision making may be difficult, but indecision often is more untenable as a way of life. A while back newspapers carried the story of a unique organization in our country called the Procrastinators' Club of America. The president of that club reported, with tongue in cheek, that the members of the group planned to do their 1972 Christmas shopping right away. They had planned to do it sooner, but 1973 got away before they knew it. In addition, the club was planning to have its second annual meeting but decided to postpone it. The purpose was to elect the officers who had assumed office in 1956. They had intended to hold an election in 1957 but never got around to it.

This amusing organization has a declared membership of some 1,200, but that hardly constitutes the number of Americans who actually should be members. The world is filled with people who live in the land of "hems and haws." Remember that little ditty reprinted so often over the years:

> There are so many things I meant to try,
> So many contests I'd hoped to win.
> But, lo, the end approaches, just as I
> Was thinking of preparing to begin.

Life can go that way. Refuse to make decisions, and time will make them for you. Unfortunately, when you leave the choice process to time, you don't always drift in the right direction.

Even more devastating is the crippling effect that indecision has on us. Consider the chameleon that, by its very nature, seeks to blend itself with every kind of background. One day the little animal lit upon a Scottish plaid and died from exhaustion, trying to relate to everything. The point of that parable is clear. Many of our frustrations result from trying to keep too many options open too long. You can't be at peace with yourself if you are committed to too many directions at the same time.

There is, of course, the risk of making hasty and rash judgments. Snap decisions can be dangerous, but even more disastrous is unending indecision. Nothing is more deadly to emotional well-being than living in the "land of in-between." The toughest place to be in life is on the fence. When you stay there, nothing is done, for either good or ill. Most of us could be greatly relieved of anxiety and apprehension if we could simply learn to make up our minds. You should mark that down as you plan your course on Guessology. Life will demand decisions, and, if that's true, staying forever in the middle is the hardest place to stand.

There is a third axiom that needs to be established in the matter of decision making. Not every choice will be the right one. There is a proverb in baseball that goes like this: "You'll win a few, lose a few, and sometimes get rained out." That's true not only in the ballpark but also in life. No matter how hard you try, you won't win 'em all.

That's pretty obvious when you think about it. There is no such thing as an infallible human mind, nor can anyone be sure he has all the data necessary for an intelligent choice. How many times have you said, "If I had known that, things would have been different"? The trouble is, you can't live life by hindsight. You have to make a decision on the information you can accumulate at the time you have to decide.

I know a policeman who was badly disfigured in

a fire. It happened in a strange way. One night on his rounds, he spotted a burning house. He knocked on the door but got no answer. Having reason to believe there was someone inside, he broke through the heavy glass door and rushed to a back bedroom just in time to pull a child to safety. In knocking down the door, the policeman's hands, arms, and face were cut and burned by the hot falling glass. The irony of it all was that the back door was unlocked. He could have easily entered the house that way if he had only known. But who can know everything?

Sometimes life comes at you so fast you only have time to go on what you can see. That's true no matter who you are. There are no perfect minds. All of us at times take the wrong road despite every intent to the contrary. "You can't win 'em all."

The trouble is not all of us recognize this, and thus we sometimes develop the mind-set of a "loser." Left unattended and undisciplined, our thought patterns will maximize failures and minimize victories. We forget the times we won and focus on the times we lost. That's true probably because the sting of defeat is more acute and thus more lasting than the thrill of winning. Morbid thoughts breed morbid thoughts. Soon the onetime loser begins to imagine that he is a chronic loser. He forgets that even the champions sometimes lose, and that in time even the best records are usually surpassed. Babe Ruth was the home-run king for years, but then came Henry Aaron. Someday Aaron's record will fall, and baseball will have a new hero—for a while. Life goes that way. Everyone is a loser—sometime, somewhere, somehow. It's sheer nonsense to expect that anyone will be a hundred percent right a hundred percent of the time.

This is why a fourth principle needs to be remembered. No decision is of sufficient magnitude to cause our ultimate defeat, our *total* defeat, unless we allow it to be. Navigators of those early trans-Pacific airlines had a red line on their charts called the "point of no return." Once the plane reached that position in its journey, the pilot was committed and could not turn back. This parable, so solemn in its meaning, has been expressed often in many different ways. James Russell Lowell declared:

> Once to every man and nation
> Comes a moment to decide,
> In the strife of truth with falsehood,
> For the good or evil side;
> Some great cause, God's new Messiah,
> Offering each the bloom or blight,
> And the choice goes by forever
> Twixt that darkness and that light.

Who can deny that? There comes a time when there simply is no way back, and the direction taken is the way you have to go.

But we have made a little too much of this idea. To assume that a choice is final is to presuppose that we have sufficient knowledge of all the alternatives. About a hundred and fifty years ago, an Englishman named Malthus wrote a book predicting that man was moving toward certain starvation. His prediction was predicated on the premise that population grows geometrically (one, two, four, eight, sixteen, etc.), while the world's food supply grows mathematically (one, two, three, four, five, etc.). Malthus's thoughts still haunt us, but we now know some of his facts to be wrong. There are ways to limit population growth, and food supplies can be and have been increased by fantastic multiples. The world doesn't have to starve to death. There are other ways out.

Life is so arranged that if you lose one game, you can still play in another one. It may have to be a different game for a different prize. There is an old prayer that goes, "God, grant me the courage to change the things I can change, the serenity to accept the things I can't change, and the wisdom to know the difference." A good prayer, but it can be misleading. Is there really anything we can't do at least *something* about?

Back in 1951 Jimmy Durante received the Peabody Award for outstanding television entertainment. That same year Gene Fowler published the story of Durante's life. Born in 1893 in one of the poorer homes of New York City, Durante had an unusual countenance that would have meant disaster for most people. But the little man with the big nose used his liability as his greatest asset and won an undying place in the hearts of his world. Here's the story of a loser who became a winner. Most of the time, too many of us conclude too quickly that some things can't be changed.

You think you have made the wrong decision? So what? Everyone does that once in a while. We win a few and lose a few. That's the way it goes. But down every road of failure and defeat, there are lots of doors that can be opened to new opportunities.

The real winners are not always those who get to the top of the heap. Many of these heroes get the good breaks and ride to fame in a world where everything seems to go their way. The real champions are those who may have to settle for less than the top, *but who know deep inside that they took the bad breaks and bad decisions and out of the wreckage salvaged something good*. In a world that acclaims only those who are No. 1, such people may pass unrecognized and unknown. This doesn't really matter to a person if he knows that even his little victory was won in a battle with odds so great that most people would have been afraid to fight.

The real winners are not those at the top but those who have come the farthest over the toughest roads. Your victory may never make the headlines. But *you* will know about it, and that's what counts.

No One Is Inferior

T H E R E was a day in educational circles when the IQ test was considered an infallible index to the potential of every student. In recent years, however, educators have been discovering this test to be less revealing than they once imagined. We used to believe that people were born with a certain degree of intelligence and that their capacity to learn and think remained fixed for a lifetime. That notion is being rapidly discarded. IQ scores do not remain constant. At any given time, a variety of factors may enter the testing process and influence the net results. Thus these tests are now seen to be at best only guides in the educational process. We can be glad of that. It is a somber but real fact that in past years many students were unfairly categorized, and the resulting stigma followed them for a lifetime.

The story of the IQ test should prompt us to think about related areas. We have a strange way of ranking people, identifying some as superior and others as inferior. Now that may not be so bad for the people who fall into the higher percentiles, but it has had a devastating effect on those who find themselves at the other end of the scale. A while back a tall, good-looking young man came by my office to talk. His very appearance gave evidence that he had a lot to live for, but he had a troubled mind. He had just finished a series of tests for admission to college. The results had not been encouraging. "They tell me," he said, "I just can't cut it. In our kind of world, where the premium is on a college degree, what's a fellow to do?" We settled down for a long talk. What do you say to a young man who, at the very beginning of his adult life, is convinced that he was born to lose? That's not an easy assignment. No one has the total answer, but there are a few things all of us need to remember.

One thing we need to fix in our thinking is that every person is unique. Many centuries ago a man

23

named Thomas Hunt Morgan did some pioneer work in the field of genetics. Among his many experiments, he did some intensive study with the fruit or vinegar fly. He noted, for instance, that one would often observe a fleck of red in the eye of those flies. This tiny red dot varied in size, shape, and texture. Morgan's research was long and tedious, but he finally supported his thesis with proof. This fleck of red is not an accidental happening but rather the result of complicated hereditary processes.

Since those early days, the study of genetics has taken us far. It's clear to everyone now that a common fly is not identical to any other fly. Since that is so, the chances against two people's being exactly alike are astronomical.

Consider a simple thing such as fingerprints. It is said that the FBI has on file in excess of seventy-five million fingerprints. They are so different that the department can fix with certainty the identity of any single person in that file. Yet we talk glibly about "ordinary" people! The truth is that no such persons exist. Each of us is unique. Each person is endowed with his own special gifts and abilities. Consequently, the whole process of measuring people is misleading. Many young people have had their spirits broken and have been irreparably damaged because someone thoughtlessly told them they couldn't cut it. The tragedy is that they have likely been measured against standards that Providence never intended to be applied to them. We are individuals, varying not only in degree but also in kind.

It is this fact of individuality that the youth of our land set out to affirm a decade ago. Their wild clothing, hairstyles, and color schemes were their ways of saying, "I'm not just people; I'm a person." Their efforts led to excesses, but their notion was right. People ought not to be categorized, labeled, and pressed into molds. It is a crime against the Creator to measure one person against another, and to belittle one or the other because he or she fails to fit a particular system. We were *made* to be different, and to be different is not to be a loser.

The failure to recognize the uniqueness of the individual accounts for much of the widespread feelings of inferiority so many of us suffer. We keep measuring ourselves against other folk; and, for a number of complex psychological reasons, we focus on our deficiencies. Have you ever talked with a member of a highly technical profession and discovered how little of what he was talking about you really understood? Most likely you became acutely aware of your own ignorance, and perhaps even went away with a sense of awe about the other person's competence and skill. A story appeared in a paper recently that ought to set that matter into its proper perspective. A while back a conference of specialists in various professions was held in a northern city. Some of the strongest minds in the country came together for interdisciplinary discussion. The conference ended in confusion because the people attending couldn't understand one another. Differences in thought patterns, vocabularies, and approach systems made communication impossible. Said one man in attendance, "Here is proof that when an expert gets out of his field, he is a 'dummy.' The greatest philosopher may not be able to start his own car, while the most brilliant inventor may not know Beethoven from the Beatles."

A lot of our feelings of inadequacy have this for their root cause. We compare our weaknesses with another person's strengths but somehow rarely reverse the process. Consequently, we spend our lives imagining that we are losers.

Once you get it fixed in your mind that you are unique and not a loser because you are different, you can begin to focus on the utilization of your own strengths. Many years ago there was an old minister in the Southland who had a sermon entitled "God Never Made a Person He Couldn't Use." You can dress that up in more sophisticated language but, however you say it, the point needs to be made. We all have our limitations; but it is equally true that we have our strengths as well. Historically, the most handicapped people in one way have often been the most highly gifted in other ways. For example, the first great poet in history, Homer, was said to have been blind. Beethoven was deaf. And remember that even though Abraham Lincoln was grotesque in appearance—so much so that one newsman called him the original gorilla—consider these lines from the October 18, 1858, edition of the Boston *Daily Transcript:*

> Lincoln is a tall, lank man, awkward and apparently diffident; but when he spoke, he was no longer awkward or ungainly. He was graceful, bold, and commanding. For forty minutes he spoke with a power we have seldom heard equaled. The vast throng was silent as death; every eye was fixed upon the speaker.

There it is again: A loser who became a winner.

We excuse ourselves too often because of our deficiencies. We drop out and cop out, thinking that because we can't do everything, we can't do anything. Do you remember the twelve men who a long time ago changed the world as it has never been changed before or since? They came from an obscure little land in a far corner of the world. They were fishermen, storekeepers, tax collectors, and the like—all followers of a carpenter from Naz-areth. In all likelihood, not a single one of them could have passed College Boards today. But these ordinary men became the world's most extraordi-nary people. They were losers who became win-ners. So don't ever excuse yourself from all things because you can't do everything.

Does this mean that everyone can be a winner in his chosen field or strength? The answer to that, of course, depends on how you determine a winner. In our world the temptation is to make that judg-ment on the best score, regardless of struggle and effort. A famed coach once said, "There is no sub-stitute for winning." It is important to win, but Grantland Rice also had a profound thought on this matter, expressed in these immortal lines:

> When the One Great Scorer comes to
> write against your name—
> He marks—not that you won or lost
> —but how you played the game.

Many of our visible failures turn out to be in-visible victories, because the fact is we never really know whether we have won or lost. A lot of peo-ple feel they are totally worthless because they have not hit the target in the center circle. But more often than we know, there are unseen victories of far-reaching consequences.

In mid-April 1912, the White Star liner *Titanic* left Southampton, England, bound for New York City. Sixteen hundred miles out of port, traveling at high speed in the North Atlantic, the great ship struck an iceberg and went down. Aboard ship on that ill-fated evening were some twenty-two hundred passengers. According to the best estimate, half of them died that night beneath the waves of an icy sea. Among those who perished was a man named Robert J. Bateman. The legends surrounding that tragic night report that Bateman gave his life jacket to a fellow passenger and stepped back to die. As the minutes ticked away and the waters inched over the deck of the "unsinkable" ship, his voice could be heard leading the doomed passengers in the singing of hymns.

The name of Robert J. Bateman would be recognized by only a handful of people today. But a few years ago a widely known and respected citizen of this land wrote an autobiography. In that book this friend and adviser to kings and presidents, a two-time nominee for the Nobel Peace Prize, and a man whose books have been read around the world, reported that Robert J. Bateman touched his life when he was a young man. Said E. Stanley

Jones, "I owe Robert Bateman, a simple unpolished preacher, an unpayable debt."

Do we ever really know when we win or lose? How can we measure the final impact of even the smallest talent when it is used at its best? The world is full of great people who owe their greatness to little people who used what they had in the only way they knew how.

I had to say this to that young man who sat in my office that day. I think he believed me. At least he should have, because it's true: Given time, *everyone* can be a winner if he wants to be.

Use what you have to the fullest. Providence will some day bring it to a good harvest. "God has never made a person he couldn't use!"

When There's No Place to Turn

T H E other day I had to make a trip to a town some distance from the city where I live. About forty miles down the road, it began to snow. My home is in the Southland; and, although we are accustomed to infrequent snowstorms, we aren't equipped to handle snow on our roads and highways. The Interstate on which I was driving is usually a safe and easy road to travel, but that day it began to resemble a ski slope. Intuition told me that it was time to slow down, and I eased back to a comfortable thirty-five. Back of me came a speed demon running like the wind. We topped a hill together, and then he lost it. The trouble increased when he skidded in front of me. Fortunately, we were near an intersection, and I took a side road. It was a close call, and an experience I will remember for a long, long time.

A bit of reflection on that event suggested a few very real parallels with life. We go through the world as people on a journey, and now and then we come to places where we get boxed in. Often the results of such circumstances are painful and tragic. The problem is that we don't know when or where we will encounter these incidents. An ancient writer once declared, "We know not what a day will bring forth." That's a grim but accurate description of life; and, for many of us, it is a frightening and depressing reality.

Someone recently described a friend this way: "He isn't happy when things are going well, knowing they will soon get worse. When things are bad, he isn't happy because he knows that, after they get better, they will get worse again." If you think that's a bit of nonsense, you aren't aware of the way a lot of people think. They live their whole lives afraid of the unexpected. They can't enjoy the good days for fear they won't last.

Nothing is quite so destructive to healthy and optimistic living as the unwarranted fear of the unexpected. Most of this fear has its origin in the way we think. Long ago a wise man observed, "We could change our lives if we could but change our minds." The truth of that is self-evident. The ancient adage "As a man thinks so is he" has achieved proverbial status because it is true.

The difficulty is that healthy thinking is not an easy accomplishment. In some ways our patterns of thought are related to environment, but the correlation is not exact. All of us know people who live in deplorable circumstances, and we wonder how they can be so happy. Conversely, we know of folk who have every advantage and yet remain depressed and despondent. It's clear to any student of life that happiness is not directly related to one's geography or circumstances. What, then, is the answer?

My time at the counselor's desk has suggested to me that happy and optimistic people invariably have some things in common. They stake their lives on certain principles and hold to them unfailingly. I have concluded that if these principles can be kept in mind at all times, the loser can be a winner. The purpose of this chapter is to identify these principles.

The first one is this: Life has a way of keeping one door open when all other doors seem to be closed.

Several years ago, engineers in our state became concerned about eroding highway embankments. Someone discovered in Japan a fast-growing vine that required no attention and yet grew with astonishing rapidity. The vine was imported and planted along a few highways. It stopped erosion, all right—and almost everything else in its path—including gardens, farms, and even forests. Cold winters freeze it back to its roots, but in the spring sun it comes to life again. You can burn it, dig at it, and cover it; but if one sprig remains, it will begin its relentless journey again. One farmer consulted his county agent, asking how to get rid of the vine. With grim humor the agent sent back a sobering message: "Move off and leave it, but hurry or the vine will follow you."

Now, that much resiliency may be bad in vines, but in people life can and should have that kind of ability to bounce back again. There is an old folk song that goes, "God makes a way when there is no way." It would be a mistake to imagine those words to be idealistic dreaming. The overwhelming evidence of history suggests that thought is a clear reality. Mankind has reached a lot of places where the roads seemed to end, but always some enterprising and inquiring mind has opened a new frontier. A crowded and hungry Europe conspired to open the Western world. Just now we have cracked

34

the door on space exploration, thus holding out hope for a day when one little world won't be enough. Remember, too, that in a day when energy supplies appear critically limited, we are on the threshold of discovering limitless fuel from nuclear fission and fusion. It seems to work as that old song suggests, "God makes a way when there is no way."

You will find this truth in other places. About nineteen hundred years ago, a carpenter came out of a little town in Nazareth. He talked about truth and honesty, about the infinite worth of people, and about the inherent dignity of all men. Not one record of his life suggests that he ever injured or hurt anyone. His only crime was that his goodness became a threat to those who dared to enslave and impoverish people. Those power-hungry foes moved with swift vengeance. They were determined to silence him at any cost. A cross was erected on an old Palestinian hillside, and they nailed him to it. When he was dead, they sealed his body in a rock-hewn tomb. But if you think that carpenter died that day, just look around you. We reckon time from the date of his birth; every city and town in the free world has a monument erected to him; and millions acknowledge him weekly with bowed heads and reverent hearts. Think about this, and you will find it easy to believe that nothing—not even death—can box us in.

There is always a way to go if you look for it.

If you can believe this, life loses its apprehension and fear. It means that we don't ever have to be a failure unless we want to be. Perhaps we don't know what a day will bring forth, but we can be sure that nothing can keep us losers *forever*.

There is a second proposition held without exception by happy people: Our hard times can be a means of strength.

Winston Churchill, near the end of his life, said that he had received so many honorary degrees from colleges and universities that he almost forgot how bad he was on exams in his youth. He put it this way: "No one ever passed so few exams and received so many degrees." But what a story is unfolded by this man's life! Who would have imagined that Churchill, troubled by a speech defect, would have used his gravel voice in the British Parliament to lift the world from its knees. But it didn't happen easily. He struggled with that voice until he perfected a kind of cadence and diction that demanded attention. But all of Churchill's life was that way. His story suggests a universal truth. The determination to stand when you are down does something to life. It hardens your muscles and strengthens your mind.

Not long ago a family in our city was overtaken by a great tragedy. The police asked that I convey the news to them. I was apprehensive. The mother had been a wheelchair patient for years. Few families had known harder times. Before I left home, I called her doctor and asked what I should do. His answer was unforgettable: "Tell them the truth. Those who have been longest in the wind are strongest in the storm." There is no way to miss the doctor's point. The storm builds muscles. If you are accustomed to walking in the wind, you are not easily blown over.

David Redding tells about an aunt whose favorite expression was, "It will do me a world of good." He said that no matter what happened to her, be it good or bad, she expected something good to result from it. You have to develop that approach to life if you ever intend to find peace and contentment. It's not likely that anyone will make it through this world without some share in its defeats and disappointments. If you are going to deal with failure at all, you must take a look at what good can come out of it. Otherwise, everything will be lost.

The third position held by happy people is the recognition that many of our greatest blessings are not recognized until later.

Far back in the dusty records of the past, there is a story about a young man named John Mark. Our best information is that he worked for two men known only as Paul and Barnabas. They were partners in the greatest enterprise of history. Paul, in today's world, would have been considered president of the corporation and Barnabas second in command. We know little about John Mark, but what we do know suggests that he was erratic and undependable. One day, concerned over the sloven habits of the young man, the top management fell into open dispute over his value in their enterprise. Paul insisted that Mark be dismissed. Barnabas, however, saw something of unmistakable value in the young man and refused to accept Paul's decision. Paul went on with his work while Barnabas stayed behind to nurture the young man and bring him to maturity. The world will be forever indebted to this almost unknown man named Barnabas. John Mark may well have become one of the half-dozen most influential figures of history. He wrote a book which bears his name, and it has been preserved in a volume called the New Testament. Any student of biblical studies knows that most of the rest of the New Testament is based on the record John Mark left. Whatever may be your estimate of the New Testament, no book ever published has been more widely read or more instrumental in molding human history.

Are we indebted to John Mark or to Barnabas for this? Who really knows? But this much is clear: Barnabas did touch a life that made the world different. So far as we know, Barnabas never knew that; and he lived and died with little acclaim. Often it works that way. There is always a time lag between seedtime and harvest. You do what you can—win, lose, or draw. But the Creator has so arranged his world that nothing good is ever lost. Far down the road, you can look back and discover that a game you thought you lost turned out to be a win. Some of your toughest days seen in retrospect have become your greatest.

If the sum total of human experience has any lesson for us, it is this: Happiness comes not just from traveling a clear and open highway. Few people make all of life's journey on a green light. Sometimes you will get boxed in. But try to remember that no wall is impassable: If you can't go around it, you can go over or under it.

Remember, too, that even your tough days can bring their blessings if you are willing to wait.

Living Without Applause

EVERY vocation that places one in the public eye carries with it very special kinds of hazards. One of those hazards involves the subjection of one's entire life to the closest kind of scrutiny. That's a part of the price for public service these days. Political figures must unveil their business interests, past and present, along with all their ties to public and private organizations. That's probably a good thing, but not many people can stand that kind of surveillance. There are skeletons in almost every closet, and few indeed are those with an unblemished past.

Even more taxing for the person who chooses a place of leadership is the necessity of winning and keeping popular support. For this reason, one of the most demanding jobs in America is that of being a coach in a major college sport. A few years ago a friend told me about a football mentor who was facing a crucial game. The alumni decided to get together and send him a wire indicating their support. The message he received must have warmed his heart. "We just want you to know we are solidly behind you—win or tie!"

That about describes the rugged life a coach leads. The task is almost impossible. His school demands that he win, but always on a limited budget. The alumni expect him to win, and they are not too interested in how it is done so long as it costs them nothing. The coach gets all the blame when the team loses, and the players get all the credit when it wins. That, of course, isn't the absolute truth; but it's close enough to make the point. No one receives more praise than a winning coach. But a loser, even with a winning past, is soon on the way out. No one stays in sports for any extended period of time without popular support.

It must be said, however, that to some degree all

of us share the dilemma of the coach or the political leader. The structure of society as we know it usually requires some acceptance from our fellows. No businessman can ignore his customers and stockholders; the professional person requires at least a measure of goodwill from his clients or patients; and the housewife leads a miserable life without some rapport with the neighbors. It is a rare person who can boast with any realism, "I don't care what other people think." You may say it, of course; but more often than not, it isn't true.

Many years ago Henry Wadsworth Longfellow wrote some lines which ran like this:

> Not in the clamor of the crowded streets,
> Not in the shouts and plaudits of the throng,
> But in ourselves are triumph and defeat.

The point of those lines brings into focus one of life's most vexing problems. We feel compelled to seek social acceptance, while at the same time we recognize that life won't always allow us the luxury of popular appeal. There are a lot of lonely people who feel the pinch of this conflict. They yearn for the applause of the crowd; but the paths they feel compelled to travel seem always to skirt the limelight, denying them the warm glow of praise and acceptance. That's a real circumstance for so many folk, and they ask an earnest question: "How do you make it when the stadium is empty and no supporters can be found?" Can you really find a meaningful life when you have to live without applause?

Let it be said right away that it isn't easy. Inherent in the emotional structure of the human organism is the need for social approval. Abraham Lincoln once had a general in his army who was intensely headline-oriented. He always played to the grandstand, especially if no dangers were involved. One day the general died, and Lincoln attended the funeral. Apparently the service was lavish and the eulogy extravagant. Later Lincoln commented: "If the general had known he was going to have such a nice funeral, he would have died sooner." As was characteristic with Lincoln, his humor had its point. He might well have said that most of us to some degree are akin to that Civil War commander.

A few years ago Dr. Wallace Hamilton wrote a book on those tendencies of human nature that are so nearly universal they can be called instinctive. One of these he labeled the "Drum Major Instinct." By this he meant the normal inclination of people to lead the pack. This inclination is age-old in its occurrence among people. There is a story in the New Testament of two men who were followers of

43

Jesus. One day as they walked along, they asked of their Master: "Lord, when you establish your kingdom, let us be the first officers in it." When you read the record, you discover that these men were not reprimanded for their ambitions. Rather, Jesus told them how such ambitions might be realized. Here is another reminder that the carpenter from Nazareth was an accomplished student of human nature. He knew that the normal personality needs some feeling of importance. It is the absence, not the presence, of this yearning that makes us abnormal.

This inclination explains so much about us. It tells us, for instance, why we are susceptible to so much of the persuasive advertising of our day. A magazine recently sent through the mail an appeal for subscriptions. The pitch was calculated to catch attention. The letter began, "This magazine is not for everyone but for the intellectual with discriminating tastes. For this reason we are sending this letter to you." Most people read that letter and were impressed even though the envelope was addressed to "Occupant." The slightest hint that we are special catches our eye and will likely influence our actions. So much of our behavior stems from such motivation. We write books, make speeches, paint pictures, and the like. We want to do good things, but that is not all of it. We enjoy being praised for it. We seek the esteem of others because it helps establish our self-esteem. Dr. Hamilton was right. When we hear ourselves applauded, see our names in print, it is Vitamin A for our egos. Praise never makes us unhappy. We even like it when we don't deserve it.

There is nothing sinful or abnormal about this desire for approval. The rub comes when the price of approval gets too high. In every life there are those times and places when the yearning for acceptance can be dangerous and devastating. A few years ago a little book was published that pinpointed this danger. Richard Bach's *Jonathan Livingston Seagull* had tremendous appeal among the people of our day. One of the most powerful and helpful thoughts in that book was this: Don't let the crowd determine the agenda or the priorities of your life.

There are several reasons why crowd approval is an uncertain prop upon which to build one's sense of well-being. Sometimes it takes the verdict of time to establish what is worthy of praise. On the day Lincoln made his famed Gettysburg Address, another man preceded him on the platform. This man, whose name now is remembered only in the footnotes of history, was a former president of Harvard, had served as a United States senator, and was a onetime governor of Massachusetts. He spoke for two hours; his speech was hailed as an eloquent and moving address. But who knows what happened to Edward Everett's speech or where to find a copy of it? Lincoln spoke just three and a half minutes, and his speech was said—by almost every critic—to be a disgrace to the office of the President. Yet, today, millions of schoolchildren can quote Lincoln's speech verbatim. How tragic but true that a prophet is seldom honored in his own country or time. Often we win the acclaim of the moment and lose the admiration of the years.

That's the trouble when you let the crowd determine your choices for the direction of your life. People are sometimes sensitive to the wrong things. William Jennings Bryan, in his bid for the presidency, was speaking during the campaign. In the audience was a fellow who responded so intently that Bryan was sure he was convincing at least one voter. After the speech, the man met Bryan at the platform. "I'm a dentist, and I'm also seriously interested in politics. I've listened to the best orators in this country. You have the finest set of teeth of any public servant I've seen."

That's often the way it goes. The crowd doesn't always give its approval to what's important. When you are motivated by social acceptance only, you are likely to overlook a lot of important things you ought to do.

Newsweek used to have a column entitled "Where Are They Now?" Heroes of the past were identified along with the ways in which time and fortune had treated them. The column often had a somber note to it. Many names that had once claimed the headlines in every paper had been lost in the inevitable passing of time. Some of those former "greats" from other days had learned to cope with the empty grandstands. Some of them had not, and they had become bitter and disillusioned. All should have expected it, however. Thomas Kempis was right when he said, "O how quickly passes the glory of the earth." How true. When you lean on the crowd and the wind changes, you can be left standing alone.

This is the real hazard of building your self-esteem solely on outward support. It is too fleeting to be lasting. Even the winners get lost from sight in the passing of time.

The real business of living is to build inner resources. Many years ago a famed English statesman made a speech to the British Parliament. The subject was not a popular one, and his position, though later proved right, was then clearly out of step with the prevailing opinion. As his speech progressed, those in the galleries began to murmur. Soon the murmur became a roar, until eventually the man was shouted down. The speaker closed his notebook and stood for a long moment looking out over the angry throng. At last, when the halls were still, he spoke softly and confidently: "The time will come when you will hear me."

How does one manage to build that kind of self-confidence? Here again Lincoln's wisdom is timeless. In those critical days of his presidency, the future was uncertain. No one could be sure which way the direction of the world would be in the short run. Said Lincoln, "I'd rather fail in a cause that will ultimately succeed than succeed in a cause that will ultimately fail." When you live with that kind of conviction, you can make it without applause.

There is no food quite so satisfying to a hungry spirit as a satisfied conscience. An allegiance to that inner voice will hold you steady when the wind is blowing in your face and the tide is running against you. There is an old story from the days of Napoleon. The "Little Emperor" had sent his armies eastward, and they had been decimated on the Russian front. The commander there, Marshal Ney, had come home with the bad news. He made his report, holding back nothing. He had fought as long as was humanly possible. Ney knew full well that Napoleon demanded every sacrifice from his men, but he concluded his report with this: "I have done my best." Napoleon angrily inquired, "How

48

do I know you have done your best?" The marshal's reply was quick and to the point: "Sir, I could not have asked you to have done more." It will work when you have done your best. There is peace inside, whether you have won or lost, if you can look back and know you went to the limit.

The trouble with most of us is that we spend too much time seeking approval from the wrong direction. Social acceptance is important, but more important still is self-acceptance. It's a splendid thing to hear the shouts of acclamation coming from the grandstand. It's even greater to hear the applause from within. The people on the outside are interested in who wins. They seldom have praise for the loser. But a person can hear applause from within, even if he has lost, provided he has played his best.

Every once in a while amid the cheering from the grandstand, we all need to stop and ask if we could find life meaningful if the cheering ceased. If you can, then you are a winner no matter what anyone says.

When You Have to Go It Alone

T H E R E is a frightening statistic abroad in our land these days, and it has to do with the most precious of all human relationships. Last year, we are told, some two million marriages were performed in this country. According to the statistics, one-fourth to one-half of these marriages will be dissolved by divorce. Because of this, agencies designed to assist people are frantically gearing themselves to deal with the tensions and stresses of the modern home. Volumes upon volumes pour off the presses in an urgent effort to cope with the problem. Secular and religious counselors are intensely engaged in establishing every conceivable tool to head off what many believe to be the breakdown of the most ancient of man's institutions, the home. In addition to the books being published, there are seminars, retreats, and institutes being organized to bring marriage partners together for specialized help. These efforts are meeting with some success, and for this all of us can be thankful.

Henry Grady, the great southern newspaperman, declared that he once stood on the steps of the Capitol in Washington thinking that he was at the heart of America. But further reflection suggested to him that the heartbeat of this country cannot be localized in such a place, no matter how majestic and impressive the Capitol may be. The heart of the country, he decided, is the home. When it fails, so will the country. Grady's position is supported by the collective experience of all major civilizations. Adolf Hitler once imagined that people could be bred as animals. The children could then be removed from the environment of the home and reared as wards of the state. But Hitler's one-thousand-year Third Reich is no more, and not the least of the forces that did it in was his mistaken notion of the unimportance of the home.

When all of this is said, however, the fact remains that divorce is real; and millions of Americans are having to go it alone. Homes come apart, the efforts and resources of skilled people notwithstanding. In the place where I work, we have a counselor who is trained professionally and by experience to work with the gamut of human problems. The waiting room to his office is often filled with people who are trying with little success to salvage their marriages. Sometimes the number of conferences with these people runs into the dozens. They are referred to all kinds of specialists from medical advisers to experts in family budget planning. Yet, despite the endless hours of attention, the efforts seem futile. Many homes are divided, and the partners finally have to go their separate ways.

Sometimes one gets the feeling that, when the end comes and the divorce court has done its work, the people affected are forgotten. That's a sad commentary on our concern for human need. In recent years more and more agencies are recognizing the problem and are attempting to help these "new loners" deal with one of life's most frustrating failures. The problems are so complicated it is folly to expect that one short chapter in a small book could even probe the surface. But perhaps what we can do is to look at a few things that will lend some encouragement to people who have to deal with the wreckage of a broken home. Perhaps, too, these few pages will prompt those involved to seek—if necessary—further assistance in dealing with their frustrations.

Any commentary on this matter must begin with the recognition that marriage is a sacred, time-honored institution, and the dissolution of it is inevitably painful. This is crucial in dealing with the problem of divorce. In recent years our attitude toward marriage has become so casual that we can easily imagine the dissolution to be no more than a trifle. A recent story making the rounds is about a woman who said to a friend, "My husband is impossible. He irritates me so much I'm even losing weight." "Why don't you leave him?" inquired the friend. "I plan to," came the response, "just as soon as I lose fourteen more pounds." If there is any humor in that, it should never overshadow the story's more serious implications. We have sized up marriage in our times to be nothing more than a convenient arrangement. When it is no longer convenient to our purposes, we simply get out.

But getting out is not that easy to handle. In the wedding ceremony there is usually this sentence: "Marriage is a holy estate, instituted by God." Now, this is not puritanical moralizing handed down to us by less enlightened generations. Rather it is the faithful description of creation's intended scheme of things. Marriage is a sacred relationship, carved by the Creator into his prevailing plan; and

53

to run counter to this design is not without penalty. All human experience stands in support of this, and the evidence is that no home is ever broken without someone's getting hurt—often everyone, including innocent people. This is why serious attention needs to be given to the appropriate conduct and attitudes for partners in the home. Marriage is not just a human plan; it is a part of a deeper scheme. When that design is ignored, there is corresponding suffering.

We need to be fully aware of this whether we are the victim or the observer of a broken home. No human experience, including death, can be quite so painful. Frequently those involved declare, "I'd rather be dead than go through this." That is not just a figure of speech but often a genuine wish. The incidence of suicide and homicide erupting from an exploding home is of grave concern to any counselor. If pain can be that severe, then it must never be taken lightly. This needs to be said to those experiencing the trauma. You can expect hurt when your marriage breaks up, and the fact that you are hurt is not the exception but most likely the rule. It helps to be aware of this, and it also helps if those to whom you turn for assistance understand the hurt. They are less likely to be offended by your possible emotional outbursts. It is less likely, too, that valuable time will be wasted in censure and reproach. There are occasions when people need to be reminded of their mistakes. But when a marriage has come apart and all alternatives have been exhausted, broken hearts need compassion and understanding.

Dr. Leslie Weatherhead has a little parable that makes a valid point. He told of a steward aboard a transatlantic ship who seemed to be preoccupied and was often inattentive to his duty. The passengers were impatient and made no effort to restrain their anger. What they did not know was that, a few days out of port, the steward had received word of his wife's death. It helps to understand the hurts of others. If we did, we would be more compassionate and tolerant. This is needed therapy for every wounded spirit, and it is especially crucial for those who for any reason are having to go it alone.

However, when we have recognized the sacred character of marriage and the hurt resulting from its dissolution, another step needs to be taken by those involved. We must face the inescapable fact that preoccupation with the past is deadly. It's a perfectly human inclination to respond to hurt first with self-pity and then with resentment. Our initial reaction to any painful circumstance is, "Why did this happen to me?" Sometimes we can ferret out answers to that question, but most often we cannot. We have not yet identified all of the reasons for human suffering and probably never will. In any case, whether or not we can actually establish the cause for our hurt, the human mind moves quickly from self-pity to resentment—resentment toward people who may conceivably be responsible for our difficulty. Only with the most rigid self-discipline can we avoid these reactions. Unfortunately, the failure to exercise this discipline can be totally destructive.

There is a curious sentence in one of the world's oldest books: "If any man compels you to go one mile with him, go with him two." That's a strange instruction until you understand the background from which it came. The reference was to an old Roman law that permitted a Roman soldier to require civilians to carry the soldier's pack for a distance of one mile. The subjected people deeply resented this humiliation. Their tempers smoldered in pent-up fury. They kept asking, "Why must we be victimized by such inhuman treatment?" Of course, they should not have been. But at the time and place this instruction was written, there was little that could be done about it. The result was that the people were becoming bitter, wasting their energies in useless anger. That is why this instruction was given to them: "Don't destroy yourself in futile antagonism. What you can't help, you accept. Resentment is self-destructive. You do what you can constructively, and then learn to live at peace with the rest."

That's sage advice, and never more appropriately remembered than in the upheaval and conflict that results when people are estranged from one another. The temptation is to settle accounts for any injustices, to continually agitate old wounds, and to nurse grudges. It isn't easy to avoid this, but no wounded spirit can regain its health until this temptation has been conquered.

We ask, of course, if there is any way to avoid these feelings of resentment and bitterness. The remedy will vary from individual to individual. It helps to remember that, in the final analysis, revenge is both impossible and unnecessary. A friend reports that as a boy he was mistreated by another lad. This friend said that he decided to even the score by carrying some burrs in his pocket and, when the opportunity presented itself, to use them to scratch the boy who had hurt him. But he discovered that, while he was carrying the instruments of torture, he succeeded only in scratching himself. It usually works that way. Revenge for the most part injures the avenger more than the avenged.

Too, why such revenge anyway? A friend of mine has a pithy little saying that's more than half-true. "The sun doesn't shine on the same dog every day!" That's homespun wisdom, but it does suggest that, after a while, the inevitable and relentless processes of justice work through to their own conclusion. There is a better way to use one's energies than in the fruitless effort to get even. So why keep on reliving the past? If you can't go back, then the best way to go is forward.

This is why the most important thing remaining to be said is this: *You have to make the best of what's left.* Roy Putnam related in a recent book, entitled *Life Is a Celebration,* an incident out of the life of Bill Klem, one of baseball's most colorful and celebrated umpires. Klem was powerful and aggressive and totally in charge when he was behind the plate. It was the ninth inning in a crucial game. The batter put the ball in left field, and the third-base runner streaking for home collided with the catcher and everyone else at home plate. The players in one dugout yelled, "He's safe!" while the other side shouted, "He's out!" Klem was standing at the plate when the dust cleared. His fist was raised as he shouted back so that all could hear, "He ain't nothing 'til I've called it!"

Move this story over into life, and it stands for something we need to remember. Life isn't anything until we have decided what it's going to be. It would be great if we could stack the deck and always get the cards we want. But no one has ever successfully managed that. Life is taking the bad hands dealt to you and making the best of them.

One of the oldest parables in the world is about a man who went to a potter's house to watch the workman as he fashioned his earthen vessels. As the clay turned on the wheel, the potter's hand slipped and the intended design was marred. The potter, however, did not throw the clay away, but took it in hand again and worked with it until he made something useful. There are many lessons to be gleaned from this age-old story. Among them is this: There are infinite opportunities to redeem the past into a usable future. Nothing we have ever done, or that can ever be done to us, can prevent that. There is always a door that will open when every door seems closed. When you can't go back, then you must go forward.

The trouble with so many people who have to go it alone is their belief that their shattered world will be and must forever be shattered. That isn't true. There is never a storm so violent but that it is followed by the sunlight. The business of life is to manage survival until the storm subsides. You then pick up the pieces and find a way to put them together again. That is difficult; but when you get down to it, the alternatives are limited. You can wallow in self-pity and burn yourself out in resent-

59

ment and anger. But that makes for very miserable living. So why not use the same energies looking for a new door to a new life?

John Wooden's motto is forever right: "Things turn out best for those who make the best of the way things turn out."

Stuck with the
Wrong Job

I N California a few years ago, there was a professional basketball team involved in one of those end-
of-the-season player exchanges. A Los Angeles
sports editor picked up the story for his paper. The
next morning the story appeared under the headline LOCAL TEAM LANDS STAR AND A SECOND-STRING
PLAYER. There was a minister somewhere in the
vicinity who read the headline. He wrote a sermon
on the theme, and that sermon has had wide distri-
bution across the land. The title of it was "When
You Are Not No. 1." The question the minister

asked was "How would you react to being called 'second-string'?" What about your wife or son having to say, "That's my husband [or father]. He's just second-string"?

That question is not just theoretical for many of us. We have experienced it firsthand and understand the feelings it creates. We've heard the old saying "There is plenty of room at the top." Whoever said that was not quite in line with the reality of things. The fact is, the top—or at least the road to it—is crowded. The nearer you approach the top, the more strenuous the competition becomes. Because of this, most of us are destined to take our places alongside the second-string players. We do not accept that place willingly or with grace. Most of us attempt some resistance against the sidelines. No one likes to be called "second-string."

One of the reasons so many young people today have trouble selecting their vocations becomes apparent here. Everyone wants to choose a walk of life that will give some chance at distinction. The trouble is that the options are so many and the variables so numerous that a lot of youth are baffled and bewildered by the problem. The result is that a vocation may come not as a matter of deliberate choice, but as a sort of hit-or-miss proposition decided more by happenstance than anything else.

Along with this problem there is another related

to it. There are those who, having made some effort at conscious choice, discover in later years that their choice was not the right one. Almost every day the person engaged in counseling meets someone who feels caught in a job role he or she doesn't enjoy. Such people are, however, trapped by time and economics and see no choice but to tough it out to the end. Every hour on the job for them is a matter of drudgery and dread. "If only I had gone down another road," they say. "But it's too late now." Isn't this the way a lot of people you know feel about their work? They either did not know how to make the choice, or they feel they made the wrong one. When you list the problems that most frequently trouble people, the matter of vocation will rank near the top. Millions of people ask, "What am I supposed to do with my life?"

This question needs a skilled answer. In recent years we have devised a whole series of evaluation tests to aid us in this problem, tests that supposedly enable us to find our aptitudes and choose a comfortable and appropriate vocation. But so often even the most careful analysis is of little value. That's especially true in these days when the job market is so uncertain and when long-established vocations are undergoing such radical and frequent changes. About the only thing left for many people is to take a new look at where they are and try to make

63

the best of it. Perhaps we can offer a few ideas that have proved helpful to many people who are grappling with such problems in their life's work.

Perhaps the first thing that should be remembered is this: Whatever one's choice of vocation may be, it should be consistent with one's particular talents and aptitudes. Recently in a national magazine, there was a story about a student who, on his first day at college, was asked to write a theme on the story of his life. A few days later the professor returned the papers with grades and comments. This particular student entered an immediate protest. He had been given a C+. "What right," he demanded, do you have to rate my life a C+?"

Of course, the professor had something else in mind when he graded the papers. But the fact is, many of us *do* have C+ lives. Rarely is anyone endowed with an overabundance of exceptional gifts, and even the most exceptional people have their share of deficiencies. Most of us think of ourselves as ordinary people with average talents. Because of this, we imagine that life for us will always be less than spectacular.

One of the most challenging things about life, however, is that its fullest meaning is derived not from being exceptional, but from the faithful use of what we do have. In the New Testament, there is a little story that suggests this truth in a simple but splendid way. It is a story about a man who had to make a trip, and while doing so entrusted his property to three faithful employees. In the story we're told that the man gave five "talents" to his first servant, two "talents" to the second, and one "talent" to the third. The word "talent" originally meant a fixed amount of money, but because this parable has become so widely known and retold through the centuries, it has given a key word to our language—*talents*, meaning one's abilities or aptitudes. You will remember that the five-talent man doubled his money while the master was away, and the two-talent man did the same, but the one-talent man buried his money in the ground.

A lot has been said about the five-talent man and the man with the one talent, but very little has been said about the fellow who received two talents. Yet we should consider him because the second man—the middle man—is the one more nearly akin to the majority of us. He was neither brilliant nor dumb, highly talented nor incompetent. He was simply the average fellow with ordinary aptitudes. When you read his story, however, you will discover that he used what he had wisely; and even though he was limited, his reward and satisfaction from the fulfilled trust was exactly equal to the reward received by the man who got far more. We should never miss the point of this story, which is

65

that you can gain as much joy from using what you have to the fullest as does the fellow who has been given more.

Sometimes we have the mistaken notion that satisfaction in life is dependent upon our achieving some important place of distinction. It should be fairly evident to us that such is not the case. The incidence of suicide, for instance, is not confined to the "down-and-outers," but is also frequently present among "up-and-outers." Inner satisfaction is not guaranteed simply because you arrive at the top. Indeed, sometimes the stars can be more tormented and troubled than the "second-stringers." Inner peace has more to do with the faithful utilization of one's gifts than with the quantity of gifts one possesses.

Recently I talked with a young man who had failed an important examination. He described it in his own vivid way: "I busted it, but it doesn't bug me. I gave it all I had and could not have done better if you had held a gun on me." This lad had discovered an important truth. Inner satisfaction can result when you have done all you can with what you have.

Once you understand that inner peace results from the proper utilization of your aptitudes, then a second idea must be considered: Whatever you do as your daily work, it must be meaningful. A long time ago someone wrote a sentence that should be remembered as a timeless and workable principle: "Meaning in one's work does not come from the occupation but from the worker." In other words, the task is not so much to find meaningful work as to find meaning in whatever we do.

That's not easy, but it *is* possible. There is a story about a fellow who asked his nephew if he was in the top half of his college class. "No," answered the boy. "But I am one of those fellows who make the top half possible." That story is close to the point. It takes a bit of ingenuity sometimes to find any significance to what you are doing; but if you are innovative, it can be done.

Carlyle once wrote, "Blessed is he who has found his life's work. Let him ask no further blessedness." That's an admirable position in which to find oneself. If we have vocations that consistently frustrate us, then perhaps we should change. But some people can't change, and their only choice is to "bloom where they are planted." If you are in a vocation not intrinsically rewarding and you can't change, then the only way out is to find meaning to life where you are.

It is amazing how many people are able to do this. There is a little plaque often sold in novelty stores to be used on the walls of kitchens. It has this written on it:

Lord of all pots and pans and things,
Since I've not time to be a saint by
Doing lovely things or watching late
With thee or dreaming in the dawn light
Or storming heaven's gates, make me a
Saint by getting meals and washing up the plates.
Warm all the kitchen with thy love and light
It with thy peace. Forgive me all my worry and
Make my grumbling cease. Thou who didst love to
Give men food in room or by the sea
Accept this service that I do.
I do it unto thee.

The author is not identified on the plaque, but, whoever it might have been, such a person could likely find meaning in any kind of work. It is conversely true that without that kind of perceptiveness, even the most exciting vocation would become dull and meaningless.

Many of us continue to believe that the grass is greener on the other side of the fence. If we could change our geography, our identity, or our circumstances, life would be better. Sometimes that's true, but it is never true if you carry your problems with you. Often the people who find life most meaningful find it where they are. Saint Paul gained the pinnacle of history while serving a jail sentence. Jesus claimed the attention of the ages from the dusty trails of Galilee. The key to life is not to find a meaningful place, but to find meaning in the place where you are.

How do we achieve this? To answer this question, we need to ponder a third idea. The key to finding meaning where we are is to find ourselves useful in something outside ourselves. A widely known weatherman from Philadelphia spoke at a North Carolina college recently. He said that he often felt ashamed that his job had such a poor-sounding title. He went on to say that he had gone to New Jersey the previous Thanksgiving Day to have dinner with some senior citizens. They made such a fuss over him that he thought it was because they had seen his face on television. But one man— way into his nineties—came over and said, "Son, we are making a celebrity of you not because you are on television but because you are the weatherman. At our age the weatherman is the only fellow who promises us a tomorrow." Said this weatherman, "I've felt differently about my job ever since. It's taken on new meaning."

That's a homely example of a serious point. When you realize that what you do makes a difference for good in the lives of others, then what you do takes on new meaning. We need to remember that some men draw plans for a cathedral, some compose music for its organ, while others cut the stones and build the road to its door. Yet each is essential in the total enterprise.

Friedrich Nietzsche once said that having a "why" to live for enables one to endure any kind of "how." The devastating burden that grinds most of us down is a life that works itself out to no useful purpose. You have to find something to give yourself to, something that leaves you with a feeling of usefulness, if life is to be worthwhile. If you can't find it in your vocation, then find it in your avocation. If life is to be satisfying, you have to feel that you count for something.

Teddy Roosevelt was right when he said that life belongs to the man who is actually in the arena —whose face is stained by the dust and sweat and blood. It belongs to those who try and fail, and rise to try again. Life is found by those who spend themselves for worthy causes; and even if they fail, they fail while daring greatly.

This is still true: When you ask, "What am I supposed to do with my life?" the answer is always, "Something useful." The saddest people on this earth are not those who are overworked but those who have nothing worthwhile to do.

Forced to Slow Down

A FEW years ago most Americans were shocked to find themselves in the middle of a gasoline shortage. For years we had driven up to the service station and said to the attendant, "Fill 'er up." We would then race away on our errands scarcely aware that we were using up a limited energy source. When the gasoline crisis came, the reaction was widespread and immediate. Strict conservation measures were invoked all across the country, and automobiles were lined up for blocks as people sought to purchase a few gallons of the precious fuel.

One of the measures arising from the shortage was a sharp reduction in the speed limit. It took a bit of getting used to, but recent surveys suggest that most Americans now believe that the fifty-five-mile-an-hour speed limit should be retained. Traffic injuries and fatalities have been considerably reduced in almost every part of the country, and property damage as a result of accidents is decidedly down. In addition to these fortunate benefits, driving for many people has become far more enjoyable. At last many of us are seeing the gorgeous scenery along our nation's highways.

Most thoughtful people in reflecting on this situation have wondered if it might not be a good thing if all of life were more limited in its pace. We live under the pressure of time schedules and packed calendars and find ourselves with too many places to go and too many things to do. A few years ago a native of southern Appalachia spent some time observing the tourists visiting his lovely homeland. As he saw these people rushing to and fro, even on vacation, he exclaimed to one of them, "Why don't you slow down? You're gonna run by more than you'll ever catch!" The wisdom of that quaint observation is evident. In our frenzied haste we do pass by many things that need our attention.

There is in the Southland an editor who publishes a magazine directed toward professional and managerial people. Recently, in describing his readers, he stated that they make good salaries and live in comfortable well-to-do neighborhoods; however, they feel harassed, overworked, and continually pressured for sufficient time to complete their responsibilities. On the whole, these readers feel compelled to spend limited time with their families and often experience acute guilt over the little contact they have with their children. Most Americans feel some kinship with such people. We have become slaves to the famed American success story. We feel we have to get to the top, regardless of the price. We sacrifice our health, our families, and our personal well-being to that goal.

When you examine what goes on in the minds and hearts of many of those who aim for the top, the discoveries are both surprising and disturbing. In many instances they aren't very happy people. Many of them feel caught in an ever-tightening spiral from which there seems to be no escape. Hemmed in by a life-style that feeds on itself, they live their whole lives at a frightful and dizzy pace. They feel pulled in too many directions, unable to give their full attention to anything. They worry not only about what they must leave undone but are also concerned about the quality of work they

73

are able to do. They rarely have enough time to do anything well. They live their lives at top speed and on the ragged edge of desperation.

Now, the danger of this life-style is not only what happens to these people physically but also what happens to them mentally and emotionally. Almost invariably such people develop a strange mind-set. It can be labeled the "someday syndrome." We mean by this the projection of meaningful life into some hazily defined future. The victims of this syndrome plan to enjoy life at some future date—the precise point never being quite identified. They talk about the time when their families will need fewer things, and when they will no longer be pressed by the demands these and other requirements make upon them. They imagine that life will be different when they get their next promotion or will be easier when they retire. The trouble is that the someday syndrome becomes habitual, to the point where there is always a reason to postpone the someday to the next day.

For some people there comes a reduction of pace that is not optional, and the someday syndrome has to be abandoned. Countless Americans for one reason or another are under mandate to slow down. If life is to have its richest meaning, it has to be found today. Some have experienced the infirmities of later years and must lead more sedate lives simply because of sheer limitations of physical strength. There are others who even in their youth and middle years have for medical reasons been compelled to drop their personal speed limit. Heart attacks, accidents, and other severe health problems take their toll among all ages. When these limitations strike, almost always there are psychological adjustments that have to be made.

Those who have never experienced such situations can scarcely understand how radical are the adjustments that follow. In many instances, those afflicted undergo an initial season of depression. That is understandable. People who have been accustomed to running at high speeds suddenly find that much of what they have been doing must be curtailed. The feeling that sweeps over them is akin to the disappointment that comes to a runner who has lost a crucial race. It's the old feeling of being a loser; and in some instances, the victims feel permanently barred from ever running again.

Yet anyone who works with such people will often make a pleasant discovery. After the initial shock of the handicap has passed, many of those afflicted find life even more exciting than before. As the driver who has rushed for years along a certain highway suddenly discovers its lovely scenery when he is forced to drive slower, so do these "limited runners" find a new life when the pace is less taxing.

Several years ago Mac Davis recorded what became a hit song. It had a delightful melody, and one line in the lyrics ought to haunt all of us: "You gotta stop and smell the roses every day." Davis was trying to tell us that our days are not without number, and no one knows how many or how few they are. If you don't have time to see the lovely things as you pass them, you are traveling too fast. That's good advice for everyone, especially those hard-driving people intent on reaching the top. If you are missing the roses, you are missing everything. "Someday" often has a way of coming too late.

Many people who have been put out of the race by some limitation report that they have learned the significance of this. They find beauty where they never expected it, roses where they had never had time to look. No one who learns that is really a loser.

Another thing you discover among these sloweddown runners is a new appreciation for people. It's easy in a push-and-shove world to utilize people as tools for achieving objectives and goals. When people are used for such purposes, then meaningful relationships are impossible to establish. One of the severe problems that people of great eminence have to handle is coping with loneliness. Their friendships are often superficial, based on status and position. In every situation, even social functions, there is a competitive atmosphere devoid of sincere trust and concern. Many have learned the sad truth of that timeless proverb, "It can be lonely at the top."

Some people have the ability to master this potential hazard of success. It is said that when Marconi invented wireless telegraphy, it was so mysterious that adults did not understand it, to say nothing of children. One day a little boy came to the famed inventor's impressive headquarters. He asked to see the "master of the house." When he was ushered in at Marconi's insistence, the boy said: "I want you to use your machine to talk to God. My dog is very sick. My father says we must send him back to heaven, and I want God to let me keep him." Marconi did not tell the little boy that his invention would not work for such purposes. He sent the boy home, promising to do his best. Then, as busy as he was, he found one of the finest veterinarians in London, who was able to save the puppy. Those who knew Marconi report that he was that kind of man. He never ran so fast that he had no time for people.

Simple kindness is not a quality reserved only for people of leisure. Some of the busiest folk are also the most concerned and compassionate. It's not so much the limitations of time as our inner attitudes that determine our approach to others. People who are concerned with human beings find a way to fit those concerns into busy schedules. After all, courtesy and kindness are not excessively extravagant in their time requirements. But in any event, the time involved brings rewards far beyond the time effort expended. You don't have to drop out of the race to care about others. If you do, you are running in the wrong race.

People who have been forced to limit speed frequently report that interpersonal relationships grow deeper and more meaningful simply because there is more time to cultivate them. Much of the tension of competition has been removed from those relationships. There is a sense of appreciation for what people *are* in themselves, rather than for the power they may wield or exert. The experienced counselor has heard it many, many times: "I never knew what good friends meant until I became ill." No one who possesses the treasure of friends is a loser.

One other thing to be observed about the sloweddown runner is his ability to distinguish worthwhile goals. Wallace Hamilton tells somewhere of a little boy who, one lovely summer day, was chasing a butterfly, a beautiful, colorful insect with richly patterned wings. The boy ran back and forth slapping the air with his hands, trying to grasp the butterfly. Finally he caught it, and a look of triumph crossed his face as he closed his hand. But when he examined his unclenched fist, the look of victory gave way to one of dismay. There in his hand he did not find those lovely and intricately designed wings, but only the dirty smear of a disarranged butterfly. "Some things are like that," said Dr. Hamilton. "They look lovely on the wing and as we chase them; but once they are caught, we discover them not to be so attractive as we imagined."

We do chase a lot of things that bring little or or no permanent satisfaction when possessed. The mistaken impression of most Americans is that a hungry spirit can be satisfied with the mere accumulation of things. So we fashion our personal empires to provide for every convenience and to cover every eventuality. This is not to say that things are unimportant: There is no peace for people who are hungry, cold, and in pain. Yet the mere satisfaction of these needs does not guarantee a satisfied heart. Happy as well as unhappy people can be found at every economic level of life. A hungry heart can make one just as desperate as an empty stomach.

The real issue confronting all of us is to discover the goals that, when attained, bring joy and peace.

Those goals may vary from person to person; but after long experimentation, the verdict of the ages makes some things apparent. Happy people are those who, when passing through the world, have time to enjoy its beauty wherever they are. They are able, too, to find someone who cares for them and for whom they can care. They will also discover along the way something to which to give themselves, beyond and above themselves. W. Beran Wolfe wrote an essay *What Is Happiness?* He said this:

> If you live only for yourself, you are always in immediate danger of being bored to death with the repetition of your own views and interests. Choose a movement that presents a distinct trend toward greater human happiness and align yourself with it. No one has learned the meaning of living until he has surrendered his ego to the service of his fellowman.

That's worth remembering, no matter how busy you are or how fast the pace you travel. If, by chance, you are one of those who for one reason or another are forced to travel at a lower speed, then perhaps these words will have even more meaning. Because of circumstance, there is a pressing need to choose more wisely the things that count.

A friend was fifty-four years of age when he had a severe heart attack. I have observed him as he has regained his health and picked up his life again. "I have just learned to live," he said. "I'm taking time to do some things I always wanted to do. Every day is a special day of beauty and joy. Colors are more intense; the sunset is more breathtaking. I'm finding time for my family and to be with friends when our purpose for visiting is other than business. I've found, too, that there are other people in the world who have needs. I, in simple ways, can make life more enjoyable for them. In a lot of ways, I'm thankful for my illness. I've learned to pace myself and discovered that the world goes on anyway. It's great to be alive."

No one is a loser if he can live and feel that way.

There Is No Impossible Past

A N Y counselor who has been long at his desk soon discovers that one of the afflictions torturing many people in our day is a deep sense of guilt. To imagine that this is solely a contemporary problem is to be unaware of the nature of the past. As far back as the human record goes, people have grappled with a deep sense of wrongness. Adam and Eve experienced it, as is evident in that marvelous story of the Garden of Eden. In the days that have passed since that far-off time, much of history has been the story of man's effort to assuage that troublesome inner unrest.

In recent years there has been an interesting twist in our attempt to deal with guilt. We have decided that it is inherently evil and a treacherous enemy to man's emotional health. Hence, the effort is to rid ourselves of guilt feelings at any cost. We have become adept at rationalizing our wrongdoings and at suppressing them, sometimes by the excessive use of drugs. We have even attempted to establish new moral codes to conform to the most unacceptable behavior. Such efforts, if successful, can have devastating effects both on society and individuals. If we should reach the point where we never experience any shame, no matter how reprehensible our behavior, then our existence and that of our society would be in serious jeopardy. This is why Emil Brunner once admonished us to look upon guilt not as our enemy but as our friend. Indeed, it is the Creator's gift to man to protect himself from self-destruction.

Once all of this has been said, however, the fact remains that guilt is not a friendly enemy to many people. When exaggerated to its worst dimensions, guilt can be devastating, paralyzing, and even deadly. Millions of people totally wreck their emotional health by a morbid preoccupation with the past. Thus, every day the counselor will meet some- one who has been needlessly defeated by a ques- tionable past. That past can include everything from the most heinous crime to a minor wrong in- flicted upon a friend. In any event, whatever its cause this morbid despondency over bygone days must be dealt with; otherwise, many good people may be completely and permanently defeated. The question, then, is: "How do we deal with an un- pleasant past?"

We must begin with the recognition that man is a perennial mixture of good and bad. There is a lit- tle slogan often seen on church bulletin boards: "There is no saint without a past and no sinner without a future." The first phrase in that sentence accurately describes circumstances as they are. In re- cent years the writing of biography has been inter- estingly different. In the past many of the records of the great heroes were written by their most ardent admirers. Often these admirers romanticized the virtues of their heroes and neglected to men- tion their imperfections and blemishes. The new biographies are telling the whole story, and we are discovering another side to some of our most cher- ished heroes. It has been a bit disillusioning for some who have watched the images of their idols tarnished. But we should have expected it.

Art Linkletter once asked a little girl to name

her favorite biblical character. She replied, "Noah." Linkletter then asked, "If Noah was such a great man, why did he take snakes and mosquitoes into the Ark and save them from the flood?" The wee lady had no hesitation in her reply: "Well, everyone makes mistakes!" What a little girl recognized, we who are older need to accept. It's doubtful that anyone has always taken the right road or always played the game exactly by the book.

Dr. George Buttrick once said that every human choice has its good and bad consequences, that all of our actions have both good and bad results. He used the simple example of feeding pigeons in the park. That seems perfectly harmless and good in all of its implications. Yet, Dr. Buttrick suggested, suppose down the street there is a poor invalid who enjoys watching the birds through the window. The pigeons no longer can be seen there because they have been enticed away by the offer of food in the park. This example may stretch the point, but it is indicative of the very real fact that we are seldom able to choose between absolutes. We all leave behind us a trail of both good and bad.

This is not to excuse us from responsible, moral choices. Too often we attempt to justify the wrong we have done with that stock alibi, "After all, I'm only human." Yet it is true that few if any of us manage to live our lives without any regrets. Even

the saints have had to look back on tarnished pasts—
Augustine, Francis of Assisi, and St. Paul are but a
few. Only an extremely thoughtless or insensitive
person is able to review his life and say with any
conviction, "If I had it to do over, I wouldn't
change a thing."

Have you ever read the death notice of a friend
to whom you are deeply indebted? Perhaps for a
long time you had intended to visit that person or
to express your gratitude in some other way. But
somehow you never got around to it. Doesn't that
obituary leave you with a twinge of conscience?

A lot of things in life are like that, and some of
them are far more serious. Few people are able to
look back on the past with complete satisfaction.
Most of us see things we have done that, if given
another chance, we would leave undone. Conversely, we have left undone things we would do if
we had another time around. The point is that we
are human and thus imperfect. Seldom does anyone
leave behind an unblemished record.

Guilt, therefore, is a universal feeling for sensitive people. Some are able to handle it constructively. For others, it becomes a debilitating monster
with lethal effects on their sense of well-being. How
can we get guilt feelings into proper perspective
and thus neutralize their crippling effects? Many
people have found two thoughts helpful.

First, reflection on the past is of little value except as the past serves to guide us in the present and the future. We do need to remember the past, of course. A few years ago a book entitled *The Century of the Surgeon* was published. In that book there was a description of early hospitals where modern medicine was trying to find its way through painful and sometimes brutal experimentation. Very often this experimentation, done in ignorance, of course, led to needless suffering and death. But out of these experiments many of the life-saving techniques of present-day medicine were learned. We can be glad that every generation of doctors does not have to start from scratch, that they learned from the past, and that we can profit from it. That's what knowledge is: the accumulation of past experience. The present-day apathy to history is tragic. George Santayana was right when he said, "Those who cannot remember the past are doomed to relive it." It's healthy to reflect on the past if in doing so we are prevented from making the same mistakes.

Beyond this compensation, little is to be gained by reliving days that are gone. The "time machine" has only forward movement. Its reverse gear is inoperative. No human effort can retrieve words and deeds from the corridors of yesterday. This time-honored sentence from Omar Khayyam is true:

The Moving Finger writes; and, having writ,
Moves on: nor all your Piety nor Wit
Shall lure it back to cancel half a Line,
Nor all your Tears wash out a Word of it.

Whatever may be the causes of guilt and shame haunting us from the past, we can't change what we have done. Life stands as we live it; and the past, good or bad, remains as written.

Everyone recognizes the futility of attempting to change the past. We also recognize the destructive effects of constantly reliving it. But the problem is how to turn loose from it. This makes a second exercise essential. We can redeem an unpleasant past by responsible living in the present.

Any fisherman who has been confronted with a snarled fishing line is aware of something that may be profitably remembered in life. The snarl, no matter how enormous and complicated, always presents at least one loose thread. When that thread is pulled, it begins to untangle the rest. Human problems are similar. Not one is so hopelessly tangled but that it has at least one handle that, when grasped, reduces the magnitude of the problem. Every counselor attempts to convey this thought to those who are overwhelmed by some paralyzing difficulty.

The trouble is that we want to solve our problems instantly when in most cases the problems took years to create. The slate is not that easily cleaned. More often than not, solutions are achieved by pulling one thread at a time. Such an approach will begin to diminish the difficulty. Sometimes one thread may provide immediate solution, but that is rare. More often it only reveals another thread that must be handled in a similar fashion. But persistence prevails, even in the most serious problems. Work long enough at any difficulty, and you will diminish its proportions.

There is an ancient and well-worn parable about a young man who was charged and convicted of sheep theft. As a penalty, the villagers decided to brand his forehead with the letters "ST"—meaning, of course. "Sheep Thief." The brand was a constant source of shame to the man, but he was determined not to be remembered as a thief. He began to live a new way. He performed endless small acts of kindness for everyone. In even the most minute responsibilities, he went to every length to demonstrate his dependability. Years went by. One day a visitor in the village saw the man and wondered about the letters on his forehead. The visitor asked some people nearby what the letters meant. Strangely enough, no one could remember, but they suspected that the "ST" was an abbreviation for the word *saint*.

Is this just a parable with no real lesson for life? Countless people can testify that it suggests some very real possibilities. As "every saint has a past," so can "every sinner have a future." There are a lot of people who have spent years going down wrong roads, sowing the wildest kind of oats. One day life brought them to a dead end, but they refused to be the victims of an enslaving past. Somewhere they found a loose thread and pulled it, found one handle and worked with it. Little by little, they began to put together new lives. They never managed to undo the past, but they did outlive it. It is amazing what happens to that sense of guilt and shame and to those unpleasant memories when you take a new and right direction. You may not be able to go back and visit an old friend. That friend may be dead. But you *can* do something to make certain that that same mistake will not happen again. The joy that comes from the latter effort will more than compensate for the guilt that results from the past mistake.

There are no hopeless people—no losers who need to lose forever, and no failures that must be final. Take a new road; there is always at least one open. As you travel that road, you will discover that guilt disappears as one's sense of "rightness" grows. Those who have tried it know it works.

Can You Run
with the Horses?

SEVERAL years ago, one of the leading church organizations in America made a series of television programs under the general title *Talkback*. The programs were dramatic presentations designed to focus attention on some of the problems apparent in contemporary life. Most of the dramas were open-ended—i.e., they were written in such a way as to raise questions without giving pat answers. This format was disturbing to a lot of people who wanted easy and clearly defined solutions to their difficulties, but at least those who saw the series were made to think.

One of the programs was the rather solemn story of three men on a hunting expedition. Somewhere out in the forest there was an accident, and one of the men was killed. News coming back from the scene failed to identify the victim. The three families at home were jolted rudely from their pleasant routines as they awaited final word as to which family circle had been invaded by death. The questions pinpointed by the little drama were these: How does one react when faced by such a dreadful situation? Can one prepare oneself for the great moments of stress and crisis in life?

Usually we are far too busy with regular affairs to spend much time contemplating the possibility of catastrophic events. This is as it should be. Unwarranted preoccupation with things that may never happen is destructive to healthy and balanced living. Yet, in the half-conscious background of every mind, there is the chilling reminder that a rendezvous with unexpected fate is always possible. Sometimes in the less crowded moments of life we wonder how we will respond. Is it possible to construct any sort of shelter to shield us in those days when our world tumbles in? Can we get set for the invasion of those staggering events of life?

In any study of the phenomenon of failure, a consideration of this is vital. A lot of us lose battles we should win simply because we do not make adequate preparation for the unpredictable. A prevented wreck is not as spectacular as a salvaged wreck, but, in any event, it is less painful. It is not by accident that our forefathers often repeated the proverb "A stitch in time saves nine." Just being ready for a lot of possible difficulties makes them easier to handle. For this reason such a chapter is included in this book.

In the wisdom literature of long ago, there is a sentence with some forceful ramifications: "If you have run with the footmen and been weary, what will you do when you run with the horses?" The background of that passage is the story of a man going through some troubled times. Lamenting his lot, he began to think about what was happening. Then came the arresting thought: "Suppose this is just the beginning. What will I do when the going really gets rough?"

Reflect a bit on that in your own life. You know how easy it is to become agitated and bewildered over trifles. What then happens when you are the recipient of the truly catastrophic? Or put it another way: If you can't run with the footmen, how are you going to make out when you have to run

93

with the horses? It's a good question—worthy of more than passing thought. Here are a few ideas that might help with an answer.

The first and most obvious is that life tends to move from the simple toward the complex. Historical records suggest that the question about the footmen and the horses came to a young man who lived about 2,600 years ago. Even then the world was complex and difficult. The man felt the need to change some things. He began his work in his hometown and from the beginning found himself in trouble. The people in his village resented his interference with the status quo and were determined to stop the young fellow. Upset about the opposition, he began to feel resentment and self-pity. Then came the thought, "If you can't handle the townspeople, what will you do when the whole country turns against you? Life will become increasingly difficult and dangerous. You are running an easy race now. What will happen when you meet the hard competition?"

Such a thing is not contrary to the way life works. There is a progressive complexity apparent in human experience. Ernest Freemont Tittle once spoke on this very theme. He pointed out that life is easier for us in some ways than for those who went before us. Great numbers of people now enjoy luxuries heretofore unavailable even to the aristocracy. Yet, in other ways, our attempts to make life more comfortable and pleasant have complicated it. The pressures of modern life in an urban world are staggering. Our fathers raced with horses. We run with jets and computers. Progression from the simple to the complex is a factual happening in history.

This circumstance can be particularized in our individual lives. A small child in school deals with simple sums in arithmetic. Almost before he or she knows it, those simple problems give way to the complicated equations of algebra and the calculations of physics. The intensity of the race increases with every single grade. The child often longs for the day of graduation when the pace will slacken. What he does not know is that adulthood will not reverse the process. The pressures of business and professional life, the responsibilities of parenthood, the necessary choices of every added year will all contrive to make life more complex. The pace seldom eases. Even retirement only shifts the nature of the race. Stop almost anywhere and look back: The problems of yesterday seem like child's play compared to those we face today and tomorrow.

This, of course, is not very encouraging. To know that the worst is yet to come is an oppressive threat that can stifle one's sense of well-being. Sometimes this burden seems so enormous that many people devise systems of escape. They look for a panacea—for some way to get from beneath the load, to hide from the ever-increasing demands of life. Unfortunately, life is so arranged that in the long run escapism offers no escape, and the attempt to hide finds no hiding place. The whole race of life begins with footmen and ends with the horses. Our only hope, therefore, is to get ready for the competition. Is there any way to do this?

One of the interesting characteristics of the human organism is its ability to utilize prior conditioning. Long before the study of human behavior had been reduced to a science, mankind made an interesting discovery. The ability to handle big things is largely determined by how you stand up to little things. As you run with the footmen, you are preparing yourself to race with the horses.

Psychology defines habit as the fixed tendency to perform certain acts in a certain way. This tendency can become so strong that it may go beyond the control of will and sometimes beyond that of consciousness. It is true not only that the repetition of certain acts makes those acts easier to perform, but also that habit makes possible the performance of more complex actions which might otherwise be impossible. A child will practice a music lesson, with his eyes first on the printed page and then on the keyboard. He picks out each note, painfully

96

choosing its counterpart on the piano. But a few years later that same child will sweep the keys effortlessly even on strange and unfamiliar music. Charles Kettering once said, "You don't beg a fiddle today and play a concert in Carnegie Hall tomorrow." Handling a complex mathematical calculation begins with the simplest rules governing addition. Running with the footmen is an absolute prerequisite for a race with the horses.

The principle of prior conditioning is workable in our emotional lives. Habits enabling us to master molehills make it possible to scale the mountains. Have you ever noticed that some people seem to accept without anxiety many things that upset other people? Granted we have varying levels of sensitivity, but this isn't all of it. These sturdy people have conditioned themselves by prior habit and experience to handle such things. They know, for instance, that the headlines on any given morning do not mean the end of the world. They know, too, that if they get knocked down, they can—after a while—rise again. They also recognize that some of the things that seem so important at any given moment, when seen from the whole of life, are unimportant.

This is exactly why the losers are often able to handle life better than the consistent winners. The winners get accustomed to success. They don't feel the pangs of defeat or the bitter fruits of losing. But no one can win all the time. Thus, when defeat comes, the winner may well come apart. But the loser has been down the road of disappointment and defeat. He can take the bumps in stride and carry on. This is not to suggest, of course, that there is intrinsic value or profit in consistent losing. Rather, it is to suggest that failure is not without its compensations. That's the point of this whole book. Even failure can be a success if you want it to be.

The question inevitably arises: How do we accomplish this prior conditioning? It comes as a startling revelation to most people to discover that it is going on every day in one way or another, and that we cannot stop the process, even though it is not always healthy and constructive. Take the matter of our physical bodies, for instance. All of us have friends who have to count calories, who have to exercise a measure of self-control that is unimaginable to those of us who have no weight problem. Now and then do you not hear one of these weight-watchers say, "I'm supposed to be on a diet, but I'm not going to count tonight." But everyone knows that the body will not be hoodwinked by that kind of deception. In the arithmetic of diet, *everything* counts. That's true generally in life. There are, for instance, no unimportant thoughts or deeds. *Everything* counts.

Modern psychology has become keenly aware of this as it has analyzed the human mind. The retentive powers of memory store every impression. Some are imprinted on the conscious memory; others are filed below the surface in the vast unknown of the subconscious. The sum total of these impressions determines the nature of the mind. It is becoming increasingly clear that we tend to become what we think about. When we fill our minds with the trivial and the unimportant, there is little wonder that, in moments of crisis and stress, we become bewildered and confused.

Did you ever hear someone comment, "It's too late to mend the roof when it's raining"? That, of course, isn't absolutely true; it might be better said that it's easier to mend the roof when it *isn't* raining. But in substance the first statement suggests something valid. When some devastating tragedy walks up to you and taps you on the shoulder, you tend to respond with the resources from the storehouse you have built.

Why is it that parents give so much attention to the rearing of children? We are interested not only in their physical welfare but also in their emotional and moral health. We expend vast amounts of energy and effort in teaching them basic and abiding principles. We help them to learn discipline and self-control and to develop sound habits of courtesy, honesty, and decency. Parents know that tender plants usually grow in the direction they are bent. Long after the child has left the family fireside, he will react to impressions and lessons learned long before.

It is imperative, therefore, that successful living involves some advance thought and planning. We need to decide whether man is in this world to go it alone, or if there is a Higher Power that guides and directs in the affairs of men. Building these fortresses of belief can have far-ranging effects on our lives. When the storms come—and they do come to all of us to a greater or lesser intensity—these beliefs will be our guardians and anchors. I am a minister and, thus, have an understandable bias. But I hope I am being objective when I suggest that a deep religious faith may be life's most cherished possession. I have observed that people who know what they believe, and why they believe it, do the best running when they have to race with the horses.

Learning to Wait

SEVERAL years ago a man in the Middle West published a little book with the intriguing title *Hurryin' Big for Little Reasons*. As you would suspect from the title, the book is filled with quaint gems of wisdom—many of them gleaned from the personal experiences of the author, Ronald R. Meredith. The chapters are delightfully written and are preceded by an introductory statement from Meredith's wife. She reports, "My husband never exaggerates; he just remembers big." With that sort of explanation, you can understand how some of the small events in the author's life could have been made into major lessons about living.

In one of the chapters, Meredith reports on his boyhood, which was spent on a western ranch. On occasions he would ride with his father to town to purchase supplies for their home and farming operation. Along the trail they would pass a cherry tree that had grown through a large boulder. The growth of the tree had split the rock into two huge pieces, both of which lay as mute testimony to the power of life. The story was that years before, the father, on his way home from school, had pressed a cherry seed down in a crevice in the rock. He soon forgot that unimportant act, but nature did not. Through the gentle processes of growth, the tiny seed had sprung to life. The seedling grew with such force that the rock was divided by it. Said the Kansas author, "As we passed that tree, my father always reminded me that a dedicated and directed life is a masterful thing."

Twenty-seven hundred years before that father and his son rode those Kansas trails, a man named Isaiah wrote a line that is still preserved in an old book. He said, "They that wait upon the Lord shall renew their strength." In these days of activism, Isaiah's directive hardly seems appropriate. We have labeled ourselves the "now" generation, and we are dedicated to the immediate solution of all our ills. This is a commendable position. With the wrongness of so much in our world, the brevity of our lives lends to our efforts a sense of urgency. The trouble comes when our problems refuse to yield to our impatient efforts. In frustration and despair many turn their lives to artificial "messiahs"; others drug their minds in order to make their spirits insensitive to the pains and ills of life. There is some evidence that the "now" generation is willing to become the "escapist" generation. That's a general observation, of course, with numerous exceptions; but, collectively speaking, it is a fairly accurate description of where many people are today.

As a counselor, I see people every day who have struggled with the problems of their lives and for all practical purposes believe that they have failed. The problems involve all kinds of matters, ranging from community and civic involvements to personal difficulties in marriages, vocations, family relationships, and businesses. Few of us can get things to work as promptly and as expeditiously as we want them to work. Many throw in the towel and find a personal route of escape.

If you have done this, or have been tempted to do it, there is an important lesson in that old line from Isaiah's writings and in that Kansas cherry tree. The lesson has to do with the fine art of patience.

Unfortunately, our definition of patience does not convey the true meaning of the word, or how it may be used constructively. If you will do a bit of thinking about the word *patience*, three vitally important things become readily clear.

First of all, the kind of patience that is constructive is never passive. It is always active waiting.

One of the perennial problems in understanding the wisdom of the past is the difficulty of accurately translating ideas from one language into another. Words in one tongue may have no exact equivalent in a different language. The result is that the new word chosen to convey the meaning of an old idea will impose an unintended variation in the idea. The word *love* as we use it in English, for instance, can stand for at least four different ideas in a language such as ancient Greek. Another striking example of this can be discovered in the root meaning of the word *patience*. We usually think of patience as meaning "to wait." The word *wait* has suffered a loss of meaning in translation from earlier languages. In ancient Hebrew, for instance, there are several words for "wait." Some of these Hebrew words have passive meanings—such as "defer" or "hold." Other Hebrew words translated "wait" have a different meaning. In the original versions of Isaiah's thought, "They that wait upon the Lord," the word *wait* meant to strive and to do so with expectancy and hope.

This gives the word *patience* a different meaning from the one usually associated with it. For so many of us, patience means waiting with folded hands while nature takes its course. But that's not patience; that's resignation and defeatism. What we should mean when we admonish ourselves to be patient may be illustrated by the story of the boy and girl who had some pet rabbits. While the rabbits were pets for the children, they were pests in the father's garden. One day the father set traps for the rabbits. The children, terribly frightened that their pets might be injured, decided to pray that the rabbits would not be caught. While they were praying, the little boy disappeared. When he returned, his sister asked, "Have you been praying that our rabbits would not get caught?" "Yes," replied the brother. "And to make sure, I went out and kicked the traps shut."

We should never lose sight of the lesson in that story. It is a grave mistake to believe that wrong things left alone will right themselves. Any student of the past is bound to recognize the folly of that. Historians often refer to the "pendulum principle" operative in history. There is some evidence in support of that theory. The pendulum does swing;

but if left to its own devices, its extremes are laden with suffering and needless damage. Unattended drifting rarely makes for a happy destination. Do you remember the parable about a gull that on a cold winter day alighted on a floating log on the Niagara River? As the log neared the falls, the bird seemed unperturbed. At the last moment before the log plunged over the falls, the bird spread its wings to fly only to discover that its feet were frozen fast.

It is sometimes said that history makes people. It is true that the halls of fame contain a long list of men and women who were in the right place at the right time. But a careful study of important biographies suggests that it is more often true that people make history. Many great movements have resulted from ideas conceived by a few people who stayed with them until they prevailed. Significant political changes, for instance, have occurred when a few concerned citizens have applied the right pressure at the right time. This is not to suggest that all of the fate and fortune of the future rests in the hands of individuals. It does mean that we are not totally at the mercy of factors beyond our control. We do have some hand in what happens to us. The boulder on that Kansas farm didn't split without cause. Someone planted a cherry seed. People who handle life constructively work at it.

There is a second imperative involved in active waiting. We must learn to utilize prevailing powers. That ancient writer hinted at this when he said, "They that wait upon the Lord shall renew their strength." What he meant, of course, was that there are forces that can be channeled and brought to bear on our problems to aid in the solution of them. Consider a few examples.

Have you ever noted, for instance, that it requires considerably more effort to drive a nail into the ceiling than to drive the same kind of nail into the floor? The physics of that is clear. When you drive the nail into the ceiling, you not only must exert sufficient pressure to move the nail, but you must also lift the hammer as well. But when you reverse the process to the floor, gravity works with you in pulling the hammer toward the nail; for the most part the weight of the hammer does the work. In one circumstance you are working against gravity to accomplish your task. In the other you are using natural forces as an ally.

The real secret of successful endeavor always involves this process. If we could remember this, a lot of our frustrations could be eliminated. We want to wave a wand, utter a few magic words, and make our little world right. It doesn't work that way. Most of our problems are solved by consistent effort in the right direction.

A few years back a busy schedule began to have its effect. I was getting too tired before the day was over. I visited a nearby doctor and, after the appropriate examination and tests, he declared, "There is no medicine for what's wrong with you. You build stamina the same way you build anything else: a step at the time with right habits. You learn the rules for good health—proper diet, adequate rest, and regular exercise—and follow them every day. Until you do this, your motor will keep running down before the day is over."

Who would dare argue with that? The doctor was simply stating an eternal and prevailing principle. You solve problems by consistent effort, using principles that are in harmony with the Creator's intent.

Many years ago Alcoholics Anonymous discovered this in dealing with one of man's most fearful problems. How does one whose life has been shattered and broken put it back together? Not all at once, because this problem seldom yields to instant resolution. So you tackle the matter "one day at a time." The winners are those who plod along, crossing bridges as they get to them, doing the little things right until one day life begins to have meaning again.

Everyone can utilize this principle. Take the matter of building a credible reputation. You don't earn that overnight. You win it by little deeds that in their cumulative effect gain it for you. Your word, for instance, becomes your bond. You treat others fairly and with respect. You demonstrate your honesty in little things as well as in larger things. That's the way it happens—you utilize right things consistently until your goal is achieved. Great athletes, while perhaps endowed with innate talents, cannot arrive on talent alone. They practice consistently and faithfully. There's no other way to be a winner.

The Kansas farmer was right. Never discount the power of a dedicated and directed life. When there is a problem, it's folly to expect chance to solve it. You tackle it head-on and apply the right forces toward its solution. It's like trying to get to a given destination: You have to take the right road because you will never get there traveling the wrong one. We readily admit this principle when we plan a journey. Why is it so difficult to recognize that it works in life?

It's standard procedure in golf to keep your head down and your eye on the ball. That's hard to do, especially for the Saturday morning duffer. We want to look up to see where the ball is going. But the pros know that this is disastrous as well as unnecessary. If you put the right components for the existing conditions into the swing, you don't have to look. The ball will go where it's supposed to go. Confident golfers are those who spend their time getting their swing right. They then trust the laws of physics to do the rest, knowing that these laws are reliable.

Isaiah wasn't preaching when he said, "They that wait on the Lord shall renew their strength." He was stating something about the reliability of creation. When you put the right ingredients together, you don't have to wonder about results. They are as predictable as the growth of a seed properly planted and nurtured. We know this to be true in nature. Why not expect it in life?

The passing of Mahalia Jackson a while back left all of us sad. Born in a shanty, she became one of the world's greats. Her life wasn't easy. She grew up in poverty and knew all of the anguish the black people of our land have suffered. She had a lot of disappointments. Yet she was happy and never bitter. She worked for the freedom of her people and refused to despair. In 1952 she won an award from the French Academy of Music. The song she sang to earn that award contained these lines:

> When my burden gets so heavy,
> And it seems I can't go on,
> And my pathway gets so dreary
> I can't tell right from wrong,

Jesus' voice I hear within me
Whispering, "Child, rely on me."

She did, and she found a peace that did not fail.

Life is not always easy. But when the going is tough, it helps to remember the parable of that western cherry tree. God remembers even a little seed thrust into a crevice in a rock. We need only to plant the seed and then rely on his inevitable processes. If you can believe this, much of the apprehension and anxiety about the future fades away. You are free to give yourself to the present and to live each day to the fullest. There will be times when you will think you have failed. It takes a while for the cherry seed to produce its seedling and the seedling to become a tree. But all the while it is growing and, little by little, exerting its irresistible pressure. One day the mighty rock crumbles. The secret to life is to plant the right seed and then learn to wait with trust. After a while, even the loser becomes a winner.

The Battle of
the Generations

THERE was a wistful look in his eyes as he came in to talk the other day. He had been reasonably successful in business, and he and his family lived in relative comfort. But he seemed a bit tired and worried as he said, half to himself, "It's a shame that you can't know in the beginning of life what you will know at the end." He had spent most of the previous night trying to work out the problems of a strong-willed and rebellious son. Like most parents, he felt inadequate to deal with the problem. What he wanted was the wisdom of hindsight to help him with the decisions he had to make as a father. The trouble is, as we have discussed, that life has to be lived in a forward direction and that many of our decisions have to be made by guess.

A lot of parents feel this predicament keenly and conclude that they are amateurs in an area where skilled specialists are needed; consequently, they grope earnestly for assistance. They buy books written by professionals, attend conferences on family life, and talk with counselors who specialize in child and adolescent psychology. No thoughtful and serious parent can afford to ignore these resources. Life presents us no greater challenge than that of being a parent. There are people who have a lot to give in helping us deal with the complex problems of parenthood.

One thing you learn in conversations with parents is that many times they feel they are not succeeding. Most often this feeling overtakes them when their children are coming through the stormy and stressful period of adolescence. The closeness of parent/child relationships becomes strained and seems at times to be lost entirely. There appears to be a marked lack of understanding and unity between the two generations. In our day we have labeled this phenomenon the "generation gap," and we refer to it as if it were a tragic circumstance. To some degree, it is tragic. It is always sad when people can't talk together and agree on solutions to their problems. It is particularly bad when parents and children who have been so close in earlier years find themselves apart. It's a real and valid question, therefore, when people undergoing this experience ask, "How can I cope with it?" None of us should expect simple answers. There aren't any. Someone has said that to be a parent these days you have to get used to being nervous. That isn't a very easy achievement as everyone knows. Most people, however, find it helpful to remember three things.

First, let us remember that the generation gap is a natural occurrence. No generation has ever been completely satisfied to let another generation solve its problems. As far back as there is a record, young people have questioned the experience of their elders. Even Socrates wondered about the young people of his day, and at times expressed concern over their erratic behavior. Most older people share that concern, partly because they forget the processes through which everyone grows toward maturity.

There are definite stages which are almost always evident as we move from childhood into maturity. They are dependence, independence, and, finally, interdependence. In our earliest years, we lean heavily upon our parents. We look to them for shelter, food, and security. We also rely upon our parents for the solution to our problems, and we seldom question their wisdom. They know how to ease the pain of our injuries, how to untangle our minor social problems, and how to run interference for us when the going is rough. As children, we accept their opinions and attitudes almost without question. The more secure our parents make us, the more likely we are to accept them as the central figures in our hero images.

As the maturing process continues, however, we sense an innate need to be individuals in our own right and not just duplicates of our parents. Somewhere in the early years, most likely during adolescence, we attempt to assert this individuality. We are no longer willing to accept parental domination without question. We have to seek out our own solutions and find our own answers. Here the generation gap becomes most intense. Old authorities are challenged; every notion of the past is tested for its validity. It's a time of frightening uncertainty for parent and offspring alike. The young person is anxious about his ability to fly in a strange world, and parents are made apprehensive and unsettled by their children's frustrations.

There is another stage in this long battle for maturity. Somehow the turbulent days are weathered. The new answers we devised are tested for their merit, and the gap begins to narrow. We take a new look at the old solutions proposed by preceding generations. It occurs to us that some of what they have said is valid. We supplement their experience with our own and become dependent upon one another.

This is the story in the development of every life. If the process is stopped in the earlier stages, then maturity is never reached. A lot of nervous fathers and mothers could be spared needless anxiety if they could look upon these stages as natural in the business of growing up.

There is a second thing we need to remember about tension between generations: To some degree it is desirable.

There is an old story about a bishop in the United Brethren Church in Ohio who, many years ago, wrote in his papers that man's attempt to fly was an incredibly foolish experiment and would result in failure. Even as he made his ill-fated prediction, his two sons—the Wright brothers—were tinkering in their bicycle shop with ideas that, on a December day in 1903, would give the world its wings. This story has been repeated often in history—one generation coming through where another has failed, bringing to reality what the preceding ages thought impossible.

Back in the 1960s there was a battle cry sounded

by young people all over our land: "Never trust anyone over thirty." But to believe that age and creativity are incompatible is to ignore a lot of facts. Kant, Tennyson, Churchill, and Edison reached their greatest productivity long after their youth. Many others could be added to the list. Historically it has not been a crime to be thirty-one.

Yet there is some truth in the indictment that, as we grow older, we are more willing to compromise and become entangled in the system. We find it easier to accept things as they are than to attempt to change things into what they should be. As the years pass, we lose our idealism and give way to rigid intolerance and inflexible dogmatism.

The tension between youth and parents can be creative if kept within proper bounds. We need the idealism of youth to jolt us out of the ruts we so easily settle into, and we need the experience of age to regulate the enthusiasm of youth. It would be tragic to abolish the gap between generations. The world always needs those who will test old assumptions and try new ideas. Our effort should not be to eliminate the gap, but to bridge it. This requires understanding from both sides. Not all of the past is bad, and not everything new will be good. Youngsters need to recognize that "old-timers" have done some living too. Old-timers need to realize that they haven't solved all the world's problems and that young people need, at least, an opportunity to try.

Finally, we need to remember that the tension between generations is perpetual. There is an old Grimm's tale about an aged man whose eyes were dim and hands unsteady. He went to live with a married son. The son and his wife were modern young people concerned with their image. When the old man ate, he clattered the silverware, spilled his food, and soiled the tablecloth. Because of this, the young couple made him eat in a corner and fed him from an earthenware bowl. One day his hands trembled more than usual. He dropped the bowl and broke it. "Here," they said, "if you are going to eat like a pig, we will make you a trough so you can eat like one." They did!

These young people had a son. One day they found him working intently with bits of wood. His father asked what he was doing. Yearning for approval, the boy replied, "I'm making a trough to feed you and Mother out of when I get big." The man and his wife were silent. Finally, they went to the corner, got the old man, and led him back to the table. No one ever scolded him again.

Life has a way of turning the tables on us so that at last we run the circle of all human problems. It rarely occurs to us as youngsters that we will eventually struggle with the problems of middle age, or in middle age that we will be confronted with the hardships of being old; that the rebels of today will someday be the objects of rebellion.

The parents of the present once thought their parents were the traditionalists and the "standpatters." Now they are the old-timers and the traditionalists. Someday the children who now imagine their parents to be out of step will find their children thinking the same thing about them. Understanding this timeless and inevitable process should make us all more tolerant and sympathetic with one another.

Most parents feel themselves losers at times, and some of them are. Sometimes it is their fault, and sometimes it isn't. But most of the time parents who love their children and who sincerely work at the task of parenthood discover in the end that much of their anxiety was needless. Their children run the circle and somewhere down the way look back and admit that the people they irreverently called the "old man" and the "old lady" were wiser than they thought.

An Ill Wind
<u>Can</u> Blow Good

SEVERAL years ago a little circular appeared on the desks of thousands of Americans. In that circular there was a story about a schoolboy who apparently had been having trouble with his books. His father took the boy to task and insisted that he apply himself harder. A few weeks later the boy, commenting to a friend, declared: "My dad said that if I studied hard, I would make a good grade. I studied terribly hard, and I got a D."

There are many lessons in that story, not the least of which is the danger of promising young people what we really can't deliver. We live in the kind of world where success in a specific endeavor may not always be achieved by effort alone. There are multitudes of people who have aimed at a particular goal and missed. Winston Churchill, in a political campaign, was reported to have said of an opposing candidate, "My opponent is a very modest man who has a great deal to be modest about." Churchill's humor both missed and made significant points. However limited Churchill's opponent may have been, he was at least a person. As a person he was unique in both his strengths and his weaknesses. Yet it is true that in any given contest some of us may be modestly equipped. In academic efforts, for instance, it is entirely possible that a schoolboy, no matter how diligently he may apply himself, will miss the top.

Unfortunately, either because of circumstances or mistaken judgment, we are not always able to run in the right race. Failure, therefore, is a potential and likely discovery for every human being—no matter how brilliant or talented a person he may be.

In the chapters of this book, we have tried to identify some of those strategic places where a lot of us get knocked out of the race. The effort has been to suggest a few constructive ways to respond when we have worked hard and lost. Obviously, the complexity of contemporary life and the limitations of space make it impossible to consider every eventuality. Thus a few summary thoughts are in order. These thoughts have to do with the very serious matter of facing life and handling what comes. A long time ago someone suggested three possible attitudes toward our problems. These attitudes, which may constitute our only options, were identified by three simple words.

The first word was *resentment*.

There is an old story about two carpenters who were building new homes. One day when the homes were completed, a storm came roaring in. The first carpenter had built well. His home weathered the storm and came through unscathed. The other carpenter had been a man in a hurry. He had failed to anchor his house on a secure foundation. It was swept away in the wind and rain. Now, the central point of this story is on the necessity of sound building practices in all of life. But there is another lesson here. After a while, the storm comes to everyone.

A parent who was seeing his child off to school for the first day wrote a little prayer. It contained those usual sentiments felt by parents who stand at such places. But one line in that prayer was especially significant. "Help the world treat him kindly, Lord, but not too easy. Somewhere he has to learn to face the wind." Years ago the famed Joe Louis was defending his boxing crown against a nimble-footed and daring young challenger. When the challenger was asked about his strategy, he declared that he intended to outrun the champion. Louis's reply made the headlines on the sports page. Said Louis, "He can run, but he can't hide." Life is like that too. It eventually forces all of us into the open and out into the storm. Many people don't expect this; and, unable to adjust, they retreat in corrosive resentment and self-pity.

The people of the past generation came through an era of brutal hardship. They weathered the Great Depression and two global wars. Determined to spare their children such fearful experiences, they tried to smooth out every bump. But we have learned that having too much too soon can be as deadly as having too little too late. You can't hide from reality; and if you are sheltered too long, you are often unable to cope with the vicious blasts of stormy weather and high winds.

When the first jet airplanes were built, every effort was made to make them as rigid as possible. One night an airliner on a flight from South Africa to London exploded in midair. A mock-up of the jet revealed that the aircraft lacked the flexibility to bend in shifting air currents. Tiny cracks opened suddenly under extreme stress, and the airplane broke in two. Personalities so rigid they cannot adjust to the changing demands of life come apart too. You have to learn that sometimes you can study hard and still make a D. To retreat in resentment doesn't change the situation; it usually compounds the problem. A spoiled child can't have his way forever, nor can he be permanently protected. He may pick up his marbles and go home, but he who does is usually left to brood alone.

The second word was *resignation.*

About 2,300 years ago, there was a philosopher in Athens by the name of Zeno. He began a school of thought that ran rapidly over the world. This system of thinking, known as "Stoicism," became a powerful influence among ancient people. The fundamental tenet of the movement was that the wise man will be indifferent to pain and pleasure, wealth and poverty, or success and failure. In short, the Stoics said that the way to deal with life is to fortify oneself with apathy and insensitivity. Virtue consists of conforming to whatever is, without any reaction. The remnants of that philosophy are still around. We often exhort one another to "grin and bear it."

Many of us believe that the only way to face life is to take it as it comes in silent resignation, to accept things as they are with no protest. Remember that old song, "Pack up your troubles in your old kit bag and smile, smile, smile"? What marvelous advice that seems to be. Apparently, however, it doesn't work. The man who wrote that song walked into a military canteen one night, sat down at the piano, and played it through while the crowd sang lustily. The song writer then walked up the stairs, took a gun, and shot himself. Just ignoring your troubles and resigning yourself to whatever happens doesn't seem to give life its essential and crucial meaning. Anyway, it's a dull way to live and does little to change or improve the world.

Suppose, for instance, doctors said to patients suffering from some dreaded disease, "Grin and bear it." Suppose the research scientists had said, "We will accept polio, pneumonia, diabetes, or a dozen other diseases as inevitable. Just grin and bear it. Don't get excited about such things. Take them as they come." Or suppose the great voices that were lifted against slavery had said, "Don't try to change things; just accept them as they are." It doesn't take much imagination to discover that Stoicism is deadly. In fact, it is more—it is impossible. There is no such thing as life without effort. Complete resignation means suicide.

The final word was *resolution*.

William Elliot told of an elderly woman who was walking down the street one day. A wheel flew off a passing truck. It knocked her down, bringing her active life to an end. When her minister went to the hospital to see her, she said with a cheery smile, "I wonder what God has for me to do here!"

There is a challenge in that story that seems too romantic for this hardheaded, hard-driving world. We imagine that people who are that buoyant and irrepressible exist only in storybooks. The truth is that, no matter how fictional such persons may seem, there *is no other workable approach to life.* You can resent the bad breaks and burn yourself out with ulcers, high blood pressure, and a disabled nervous system. You can accept what happens to you and stay down forever. Or you can ask the question, "How can I use what happens to me and find life creative and exciting?"

There are people in real life who have taken this approach. They have netted from their bad breaks a kind of victory they never dreamed possible.

In Decatur, Illinois, a boy ordered a book on photography. The publisher made a mistake and sent instead a manual on mind reading, magic, and ventriloquism. So Edgar Bergen got a wooden dummy, named it Charlie McCarthy, and charmed millions with his talent. Charles Goodyear was running experiments with rubber, trying to make it less sticky. One night he made a mistake and left the rubber too near a stove. By accident he made a discovery that helped to put the world on rubber wheels. Alexander Graham Bell was trying to solve the problem of the deaf and "blew it." He came up with the telephone. Shubert was disappointed in love and, out of his sadness, composed the immortal "Ave Maria." The stories are endless—people who took the bad breaks and made them into good fortune.

The point in all of these stories is that everything that happens to us can be an opportunity. Most of us drop out too soon and assume we have been counted out because we are down. What we fail to remember is that every obstacle is a stepping-stone if we have the nerve and the will to look for it. Our forefathers were almost right when they said, "It's an ill wind that blows no good." They would have been completely right if they had said, "An ill wind will blow good if you look for it."

One final word: We struggle along with what we have, where we are; and a lot of times we can't see where we are going, but we never know when a tiny seed sown will come to harvest. A while back, a fellow wrote a little article that appeared first in a church bulletin. Someone saw it and suggested that it be published in a magazine read by people who travel on one of America's airlines. There someone else saw the article and asked that it be made into a book. This is how you come to have this little volume in your hands.

Perhaps now someone who is discouraged and defeated will browse through these pages and discover at least one word of hope and reassurance. That person may touch the life of another person, and the process will go on. The name of the book and the author will be lost as a grain of wheat loses its identity when thrust into the ground, but the little seed will be producing its harvest far down the way.

This author is convinced, by both observation and experience, that we can never say we are losers. We just don't know when or where the victory will come.